TANDOOR

VIKING

The Great Indian Barbeque

Ranjit
Rai

VIKING

USA | Canada | UK | Ireland | Australia
New Zealand | India | South Africa | China

Viking is part of the Penguin Random House group of companies
whose addresses can be found at global.penguinrandomhouse.com

Published by Penguin Random House India Pvt. Ltd,
7th Floor, Infinity Tower C, DLF Cyber City,
Gurgaon 122 002, Haryana, India

First published in Viking by Penguin Books India 1995
This edition published 2006

Copyright © Anuradha Ravindranath 1995, 2006

10 9 8 7 6 5 4

Design and Art Direction: Ranmal Singh Jhala
Photography: Shailan Parker
Food Styling: Ranmal Singh Jhala

All recipes cooked by Anuradha Ravindranath

ISBN 9780670868322

Typeset in Garamond by Alphabets, New Delhi
Printed at Replika Press Pvt. Ltd, India

This book is dedicated
to
my dearest wife Kamla
an inspiration and truly a cook's cook

Foreword

Following the enthusiastic response accorded to his first cookery book, *Curry Curry Curry* (Penguin 1990), my father decided to put down his thoughts on another form of food preparation that was very dear to him — tandoori cooking. This technique, unique to the subcontinent, involves the containment of heat in a clay oven, the tandoor, to encourage the slow and gentle transformation of bland ingredients into one of the most delectable cuisines known to mankind.

Before he could complete the task, to which he had devoted close to three years, he passed away. Fortunately, along with the draft manuscript, he left behind copious notes and detailed instructions. As a result, I was able to bring the book to a conclusion in a manner, I feel, he would have approved of.

While doing so, I never felt that I was undertaking a job that had to be finished. Rather, I have regarded it as a loving tribute to a wonderful father, a great human being, and a magical cook. I sincerely hope that I have been able to do justice to his innovative ideas on tandoori cooking.

In this assignment I have been fortunate enough to have had the benefit of unstinted assistance from a number of sources. My first acknowledgement is to David Davidar of Penguin who encouraged me to undertake the daunting task of completing the unfinished manuscript.

My family members, in particular my elder brother Lakshman, rendered invaluable assistance. Sincere thanks are due to my father's friend, Durga Prasad Mohley, who worked tirelessly with me, whether it was in testing recipes or supervising the materials for photography sessions, and to my friend Madhavi who edited the manuscript.

I am indebted to graphic designer Ranmal Singh Jhala, who visualized the design concept, researched it and choreographed its realization; to photographer Shailen Parker, who gave many hours of extra time towards this project; to ceramics designer Manish Iyer for the novel way in which he created the props; and I would like to thank them for the brilliant visuals that have embellished this book.

There were, of course, others involved with the invisible work of putting this book together whom I would like to thank — my cousin Paul Flather, Dr. S.K. Shridharan, S.C. Shekhar, Rajiv Kapoor, Vijit Sikand and Moosa Sadr. Also, B.M. Pandey for his help with the archaeological references, Sunil Sud for the immaculate typesetting, Thomas and Manoj, who assisted with the photography, Salim, who ran all kinds of errands without losing the smile on his face, and the staff at Rai and Sons, where I based myself these last two years, specially Inderjeet, who typed and retyped the many revisions of the text in her typical efficient manner.

Finally, were it not for the exemplary patience displayed by my husband and daughters, I might not have been able to cope with the burden of producing this book in addition to my routine activities which, as every housewife knows, take up so much time.

Anuradha Ravindranath
New Delhi, 1995

Note from the Author

My first effort at writing down my thoughts on cooking and codifying the Indian techniques that I have followed in so many kitchens around the world resulted in *Curry, Curry, Curry,* published towards the end of 1990. I was surprised and gratified at its success. *Curry, Curry, Curry* actually became very popular, proving that my friends and family were right in urging me to put down these techniques.

This has now led me to produce a second book. But the exercise has been completely different. I have set out to explore the very special way of cooking in the tandoor.

What I offer the reader is a simple history of the tandoor, its origins and development down the ages (it was first used some 5000 years ago), followed by a series of recipes that extract the maximum (flavour) from this method. Some culinary advice from my earlier book has been repeated where it is relevant.

Once again, I have had to share the text and recipes with friends and critics, and as ever, their advice has been invaluable. This time I have also had to delve into historical archives.

My principal acknowledgement is to my friend, Durga Prasad Mohley, who has been associated with my books from the first thoughts that led to *Curry, Curry, Curry.* This time he has had to check and verify all my historical research as well as monitor the manuscript as it has gradually taken shape. Once again, I received help from his sons, Rajiv, Sanjeev and Sandeep Mohley.

My whole family, now spread across the world, once again provided loving support and encouragement for this second project. My sister, Baroness Sheela Flather and her husband

Gary, urged me on. My nephew Paul, a former journalist, again read the text from the readers' viewpoint and provided much editorial guidance and assistance.

I am indebted to the Director General and staff of the Photo Section, Archaeological Survey of India for their help.

Many other friends gave their support and help, sometimes with ideas but always with such enthusiastic encouragement that I really owed it to them, and also to my potential readers, to produce this work.

My first book aimed at explaining the theory and the methods behind the cooking of curry. This book aims to explain the past and present use of the tandoor. The future depends on you, the reader.

Ranjit Rai
New Delhi, April 1993

Contents

ODE TO THE

Fired from below
  And cascading heat from above
Made from mother earth
  By gentle hands of women in love
Charging the clay with strength
  Thou wondrous oven
Fail-safe cooker of goodness and health

  From an unknown time
Through millenniums you serve
  Now underground now from above
'Big', aromatic, baking and roasting
  Accepting grain, meat and dove
The chicken brought you fame
  And now on every lip is your name

You sit burning for others
  Calling bring your meat 'bread and dough'
And stir around me 'timber'
  Warm yourself a moment
The day's work is done
  Pay homage to the world's greatest preserver.

Ranjit Rai, *April 1993*

TANDOOR

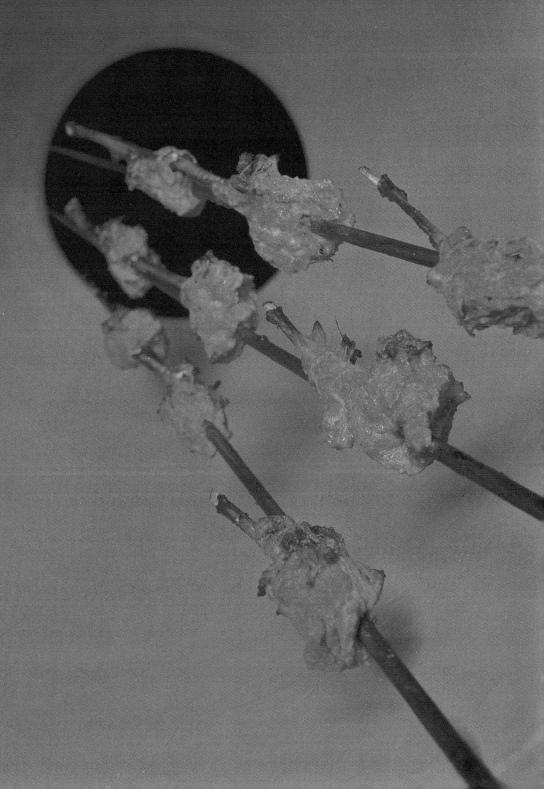

Introduction

The tandoor is an oven of great antiquity; a cooking appliance that, either by accident or by design, is extremely efficient and yet simple to make. I know that the hurried or harassed housewife may not have the time, but for those dipping into this book at leisure, I would like to build upon archaeological evidence to create a kitchen where, almost 5000 years ago, another busy housewife cooked *tandoori roti* and *nan.* Thus, the chapters that follow trace the history of the tandoor, its different names, its evolution to the present day form, its construction and all-round versatility as a cooking device. Luckily for us, while the kitchen is pure conjecture, we still have, despite all the advances in science and technology, the tandoor, the tandoori roti and the delicious tandoori chicken.

The section on recipes will indicate that while the tenderizers-cum-marinades and the masalas used are broadly similar, it is the different types of meats and vegetables, cottage cheese and tofu that vary in nature. Thus, after assimilating the basics of cooking in a tandoor, one finds the variety subsists in the product cooked rather than in any cooking technique or variation in masalas. The tandoor, with its various local names, is in use today in the Asian Republics of the former Soviet Union, the Middle East, Mongolia, China, and, of course, in India and Pakistan.

In short, the history of the tandoor and its location around the world, construction, principles of tenderizing, making marinades, basic preparations and finally the tandoori recipes are all included in the book.

Part
I

The Tandoor

*Terracotta cakes in a circular structure that could well be
a tandoor, found at Kalibangan.*

History of the Tandoor

 Tandoors have been found in excavations of Harappan and pre-Harappan sites. Where and when the first tandoors existed is still a matter of continuing research. But, generally speaking and because of the generic term 'tandoor', it is said to have originated in ancient India. The origin of the word is as fascinating as that of the oven itself. Of the several theories forwarded, the first is related to the Sanskrit word *kandu*. The word tandoor is derived from *kund* which means a large bowl-shaped vessel, either countersunk or above ground, as a permanent fixture or in a mobile form.

The kund could be used for the storage of water and grain or as a *havan kund*, to contain a ritual fire in Vedic times. The word kund became kandu in colloquial usage, and from kandu it became *kandoor*, also *kandoora*. Then the 'k' sound became the 't' sound, and so we have the word *tandoor*.

The other theory derives from colloquial Pushtu or pidgin Persian, from the word *tata* meaning hot and *andar* meaning inside. Through this liaison the word became tandoor. Thus, the two possible roots are as follows :

I	II
KUND	TATTA ANDAR
↓	↓
KANDU	TAT ANDAR
↓	↓
KANDOOR	TANDAR
↓	↓
TANDOOR	TANDOOR

How it began

If we trace the history of cooked foods, we usually think of the spit roast, on which game was cooked. And while it is not known when meats were first cooked, one could imagine that when survivors of a forest fire in pre-historic times returned to take stock and assess the extent of damage, they found a pleasant odour of charcoal mixed with animal flesh. At once, with inherent primitive instinct, they tasted the meat, and found it to be agreeable and easily chewed. This could have led to the spit roasting of game, initially on a spear, and progressing over time to a more sophisticated form of a seekh or skewer. There are, however, continued historical references to animal sacrifice, where the animal was impaled on a spear and spit roasted, the cooked meat being distributed as *prashad* or 'sacred gift'. As far as fruits and vegetables were concerned, in those early times they were consumed in their raw or ripe form, mostly uncooked.

As people began to lead a more settled existence, leaning towards farming and cultivation, they discovered leisure. With leisure came the development of ideas — new ideas regarding food, art and craft.

Bakers at work in ancient Egypt. Evidence of such a bakery was found just south of Cheop's Pyramid.

Grain was already being consumed. It was pounded and mixed with water, kneaded into a dough and baked on hot stones or what is thought to be a very primitive hearth.

At this time the Egyptian, the Mesopotamian and the Indus Valley civilizations constituting what is known as the 'fertile crescent', were just coming into their own, each developing individually but with similar basic needs. Although the tandoor had been discovered earlier in the pre-Harappan culture, it is quite certain that in Egypt the evolution of the tandoor and grinding stone took place simultaneously. It is thought that during the construction of the great pyramids, there was a sustained demand for vast amounts of food and bread. Since the Egyptians knew all about fire and how to raise it, all they needed was finely ground grain.

It is not clear who actually invented the quern, but putting two and two together it would seem the same stone used for the pyramids was used to make a quern. This could be done by placing one stone on top of the other. With freshly ground wheat and fire the bakery was born, able to provide bread on a large scale.

In India, three types of querns seem to have been in use. One of these was the rotary quern, examples of which have been found at Taxila, dating around 100 BC. The design of this quern or grinding wheel was simple but very effective. It had two circular discs varying from ten to thirty inches in diameter with an eccentric stone handle at one point.

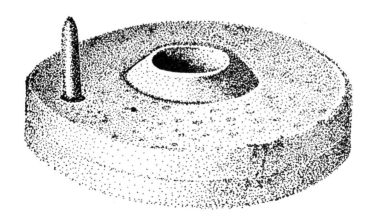

At the centre was an opening through which wheat was poured in. Some historical records refer to such grinding wheels as being three to four feet in diameter with two handles. Two strong workers were required, one pushing it halfway, and the other completing the circle in a kind of relay action. The technique produced a lot more ground wheat for dough. Once the dough was ready it was rolled out or patted into shape in very much the same way as it is done today. Then it was baked in the tandoor.

So we have all the makings of a bakery — primitive, but efficient and fail-safe as well as black start, meaning that no outside source was needed to start it and it could be worked anywhere as long as some kind of timber was available. We have the grinding wheel as the kinesis, and the tandoor as the baking oven.

One cannot imagine any other cooking appliance that could have been used in that environment. As the various elements required to make the tandoor were readily available, it became the most versatile cooking appliance and one that required no 'product development'. It has further evolved slowly over the centuries to make it more efficient, and finally, to make it transportable.

Kalibangan, where evidence of the earliest tandoor was excavated, is located in the Ganganagar district of Rajasthan about 400 km from Delhi. The name 'Kali-bangan', meaning black bangles, was given to the place because many broken terracotta bangles that had turned black down the ages were found scattered around here. Earliest excavations at the site date back to almost 2600 BC. All evidence points to its having been part of the highly advanced Harappan culture.

Many questions come to mind as one dwells on this culture, for how could people or society have been so progressive nearly 5000 years ago? This is the strangest and most fascinating part. The people of Kalibangan had perfectly planned towns. The entire settlement was fortified. The streets were well laid out in the ratio of 1:2:3:4, demonstrating a knowledge of ratio and proportions. While no palaces or evidence of kingly rule has been found, there was a central citadel area where the high priests evidently resided. This citadel area was surrounded by well-planned houses within a fortified area where rich businessmen and traders lived. Beyond this lay the lower city where, perhaps, the working class people lived. In this area altars have been found with the traditional kund and kandu. The kund contained terracotta cakes resembling our tandoori roti and animal bones. The whole scenario suggests sacrificial rites with offerings to fire, as well as the cooking and distribution of prashad.

The houses followed a uniform plan with a central courtyard enclosed by rooms all around. (Strangely, my own house closely resembles this type of construction and I begin to wonder where all those thousands of years in between have gone!) It was in these courtyards that a most interesting discovery, of special relevance to our book was made. Ovens of both the underground and overground type were found. These resemble tandoors in use today, particularly those found in Punjab and Haryana, states neighbouring Rajasthan. Along with the ovens, pits used for storage of grain were also discovered. Saddle querns, rolling platters and curry stones, have all been found. Taken together, they suggest that grain was ground, kneaded into dough, and baked in the 'tandoor'.

At Kalibangan both the overground tandoor as well as the type that is buried underground have been excavated.

While reconstructing a complete lifestyle I may add that at Kalibangan, animals had already been domesticated and contributed greatly to the daily diet by supplying both milk and meat. Milk products were well known. The art of making cottage cheese or *panir* (a dish the best of cooks find difficult to make) was known to them. Yoghurt was also known and held in great reverence. Curry stones were used for grinding spices and herbs — that is evident. Can anyone believe that they had ground spices and yoghurt to tenderize, and that they did not put the two together? I am sure they did. Looking at the other developments of this civilization, I would, in fact, take the liberty of saying that the people were highly food conscious, and had great knowledge of tenderizing and marination of meats, as also of making curries using ground spices.

Wheat was the important grain. Cultivation was highly developed and evidence of dual cropping points to a great degree of specialization. The natural conclusion is that with ovens in their houses, the availability of wheat for roti, meats, herbs and spices, the people of this culture were well-versed in the art of tandoori cuisine.

The glorious Indus Valley or Sindhu Valley civilization unearthed at Mohenjodaro and Harappa (now in Pakistan), gives evidence to the existence of specialized trade and a regular interaction and exchange of ideas with the people of Sumer and Mesopotamia. The increasing affluence and sophistication of culture is clearly visible here. The cities are much larger than at Kalibangan. An elaborate drainage system, street lighting and strict laws of building, all suggest a well-developed municipal government.

Unfortunately, because earlier excavations were not conducted with specialized care, a lot of history at these sites has been lost to us. However, it is clear that they too had the same interest in food as their contemporaries, for, in addition to the large number of terracotta cakes excavated at these sites, a bread oven resembling the tandoors used all over Asia today was excavated at Mohenjodaro. This oven measured three feet eight inches in diameter and three feet six inches in height. It has also been deduced that the old jungle fowl *gallus gallus* of the family *phasianinae*, the ancestor of the present day chicken, was bred in the Indus Valley nearly five thousand years ago. Which leads me to wonder if tandoori fowl was as popular then as it is now.

Dilmun* conjures up images of a paradise city 'with sweet waters giving eternal youth'! It was the name given by the Sumerians to the city that was an important link on the trade route between Mesopotamia and the Indus Valley.

As is often the case with trading communities, each borrows some of the other's lifestyle. Thus, Dilmun imbibed many characteristics of the Indus Valley culture. Amongst other things, there were similarities in eating habits. Tandoor type ovens have been excavated at Dilmun as well. Given its simplicity and utility, one can assume that such an appliance must have been popular wherever it went.

* Bahrain

Archaeological sites contemporary to the Harappan period where tandoors have been found

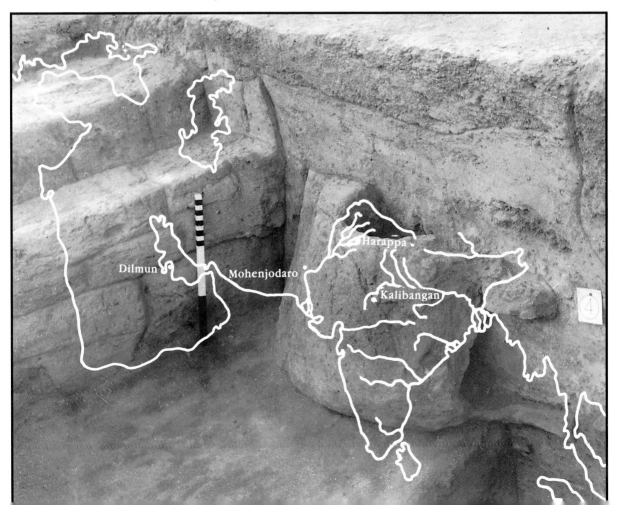

Any portrayal of an ancient culture and lifestyle is naturally open to scepticism and debate. But, consider these facts :

Sarai Nahar Rai, Pratapgarh district, U. P. (about 8500 BC).
Evidence reveals the presence of hearths.

Ladakh district, J & K. (about 6700 BC).
Cave dwellings found here contain evidence of fireplaces with bones near them. This seems to indicate that man may actually have roasted animals many years earlier than is usually believed.

Burzahom, Srinagar district, J & K. (about 2500 BC).
Excavations reveal dwelling pits with mud-plastered walls. Burnt ash and charcoal have been found in them, indicative of the fact that they must have been inhabited by human beings. Stone hearths have been found inside the pits. Contemporary to the Indus Valley civilization, this culture also had links with China, East Asia, Russia, Afghanistan and Iran.

Alamgirpur, Meerut district, U. P. (2500 BC).
A long trench excavated here disclosed platters for preparing roti. Terracotta cakes were found along with some potsherds. No ovens, but accompaniments to cooking !

Banawali, Hissar district, Haryana (around 2500–2300).
Here too excavations show a Harappan lifestyle. Amongst other things, storage jars, hearths and tandoors have been unearthed.

Chirand, Saran district, North Bihar (2400 BC–1650 BC).
The site shows us some better developed ovens, with long passages and side channels. The long passages seem to have been for feeding fuel, and the side ones for removing the ash. Here animal bones, moong, wheat and rice along with carbonized seeds of berries were found.

Sanghol, Ludhiana district, Punjab (2000 BC)
Here mud ovens and mud and brick structures were found, along with corn-bins, hearths and tandoors. More terracota cakes!

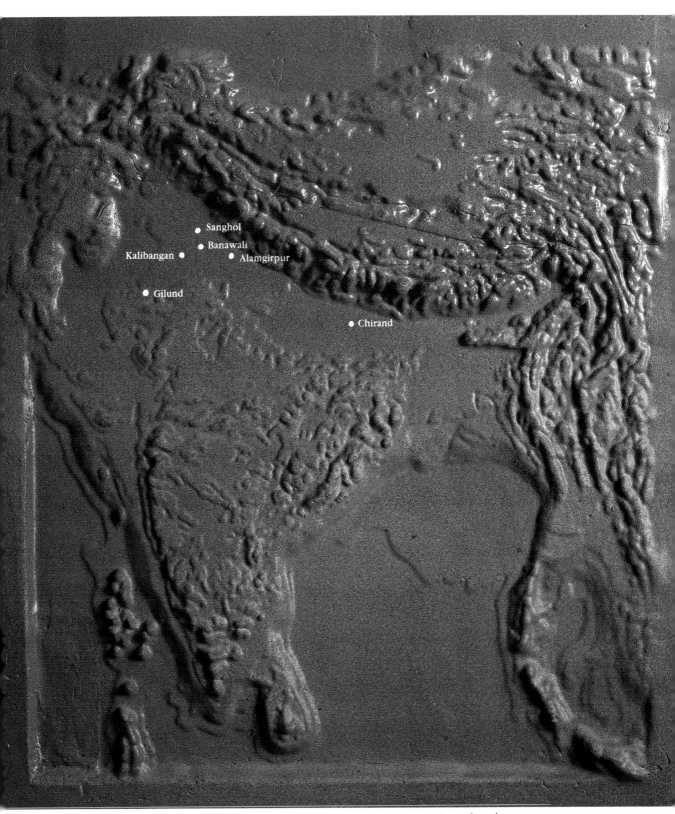

Archaeological sites in India where tandoors have been found

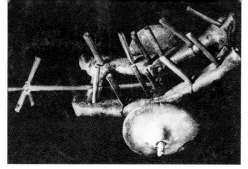

Time stands still — the toy cart found at Kalibangan could be a model of this cart still to be seen transporting grain in Harappa today.

Gilund, Raj Samand, district Rajasthan (1500 BC). Mud and brick houses with clay-lined pits have been excavated here. These pits were probably used as ovens. Alongside are larger pits, perhaps used for storing grain.

While the above facts have been arranged chronologically for convenience, there is enough archaeological evidence that points to the fact that tandoor type ovens or actual tandoors may have existed over many thousands of years.

Some form of tandoor, either an original or an evolved type, is still used all over Northern India, Central Asia and other Asian republics, as well as in parts of China and Mongolia. We come to the conclusion that between the flour and the fire, there could be no other appliance as convenient as the tandoor for baking bread, both leavened and unleavened. These breads are now known by various names — nan, roti, *paratha* or *kulcha* — but they are still baked in the tandoor.

From then till now

Following the decline of the Indus or the Harappan culture in India came the golden Vedic age. The four *Veda* or *Samhita* give us the basis of this culture: food and God — the two most important requirements of humankind and the epicentre around which life revolves in every society.

The *Veda* have given great prominence to food which is spoken of in all texts except for the *Rigveda*. Wheat, the giver of life, was considered the most important. Apart from this, the people ate rice, *dals* (*masur, chana, arhar*, etc.) and *masa* (meat), curd and butter. Ghee, the 'divine' essence of food, was commonly used. Meat was roasted on spits, tenderized by yoghurt. It was also cooked, boiled with spices and curried.

There was a notion of pure and impure meat. The cow was sacrosanct, as the *shloka* illustrates:

दुहामश्विभ्यां पयो अध्येय सा वर्धतां महते सौभागाय ।

Rig Veda. 1. 164,27

About 800–300 BC the *Sutra* describes a piece of broken pot *(kapala)* being used to bake roti. The *Ashtanga Samgraha* (AD 25) mentions five varieties of wheat roti.

Kukula pakva	bread cooked in a pit heated with chaff fire
Karpara pakva	bread cooked on an earthenware plate
Bhrastra pakva	bread that has been fried
Kandu pakva	bread cooked in a kandu (tandoor)
Angara pakva	bread cooked on live charcoals

The first mention of meat cooked in a tandoor by the physician Sushruta is in the *Sushruta Samhita Sutrasthanam* which says :

उल्लुप्तं भर्जितं पिष्टं प्रतप्तं कन्दुपाचितम् ।
परिशुष्कं प्रदिग्धं च शूल्यं यच्चान्यदीदृशम् ।
मांसं यत्तैलसिद्धं तद् वीर्योष्णं पित्तकृद् गुरुः ।

Sushruta. su. 46.356-57

He lists the varieties of meat preparations as :

Ulluptam	minced meat
Pishtam	meat pasted and made into balls on seekh
Prataptam	roasted with clarified butter over charcoal fire
Kandu pachitam	cooked in the tandoor
Parishushkam	seasoned meat
Pradigdham	meat cooked with milk and clarified butter
Shulyam	meat roasted on spits

Further, he says, articles of food dry-fried on broken vessels of baked clay or cooked over a charcoal fire should be considered light with respect to digestion. Surely the tandoor was an integral part of the lives of the people of these times.

Continuing our exploration of history, we find that the Aryans, now in control, followed the caste system rigidly. Also, that it was a concept with which people were growing increasingly disenchanted. Thus, around 500 BC, two new religions emerged: Jainism and Buddhism. Buddhist writings speak of the prevalent non-vegetarianism. Fish was available. There were slaughter houses and meat markets in Mithila where venison, pork, and the flesh of fowls and birds were sold for the table — plenty of meat eating!

Both Mahavira (550–468 BC) and Buddha (566–484 BC) were against this trend of killing and cooking animals. They preached total non-violence and called for an end to all killing, advocating vegetarianism as the healthiest way of life. This ideology appealed to the people, and gradually Hindus moved away from this ritualistic practice.

The Buddhist texts, known as the *Jataka,* are a great ocean of knowledge. In these too, we find mention of wheat roti or *khajjaka* — cakes made from wheat flour, cooked in the tandoor. Occasionally coated with *gur* (jaggery), these were greatly appreciated.

अहं यागुं दातुं न सक्खिसामि खज्जकम्प न दस्सामीति सण्हण कुण्डक विहोपत्वा ।

Jataka. 109

In Gujarat, even today the *khajjali,* a layered wheat roti, is regularly served plain or sweetened. The similarity in name, the method of preparation and the area in which it is made today, can hardly be coincidental!

The Greek invasion, led by Alexander the Great and directed at the prosperous kingdom of Magadha (present-day Bihar) marked 326 BC. The invaders managed to cross the Indus, but advancing any further proved too much for the battle-weary soldiers, and Alexander was forced to return home. It is through the writings of generals and others who stayed behind that we get an insight into the habits and rituals of the time.

Wheat was the important grain. The Greeks were expert bakers of bread and archaeologists believe that the *chakki*, or the circular rotary quern, was introduced by them. Two of these have actually been found at Taxila. With ground wheat-grain available, the tandoor was thought to be the oven most convenient for baking.

After Alexander, a period of great unrest followed, till the Kushan kings took over around 165 BC. The Kushans controlled the trade route between the Roman and the Chinese worlds, and their vast empire spread from Kashgarh, a town in the western Sinkiang province of China, to the border of Persia; from Sind, Gujarat, Punjab, Kashmir, and parts of Central India, east to Benaras, with the capital at Purushpura (now known as Peshawar). Buddhism was the predominant religion and tolerance the prevailing philosophy. The Gandhar School of Art was established. Paintings and texts pertaining to this school have been found all along the towns on the famous Silk Route.

Along this route traders going outwards from Punjab and the North-Western Frontier provinces also spread their knowledge of food to other parts of the world. The concept and the art of cooking in the tandoor travelled with them, as the oven was easy to make and carry.

Charaka, the court physician to the Kushan king Kanishka, is the author of the Ayurvedic treatise who, along with Sushruta, wrote a number of books on Indian systems of medicine. These give a detailed account of food, and of food being tenderized and marinated.

Dalhana on Sushruta. su.46.

भर्जितं स्याद् घृतादौ तु पिष्ट्वा यत्साधितं पुनः ।
अपूपादिकृतं पिष्टं दधिदाडिमसौरभैः ।
सिद्धं साज्यैस्तथाऽजाजी सामुद्रमरिचैस्तथा
अङ्गारादिषु यत्पक्वं प्रतप्तं तदुदाहृतम् ।

These shlokas describe a dish known as *Prataptam* for which the meat is first fried in ghee, then flavoured with the addition of yoghurt, lemon juice, pomegranate juice, etc. and is again cooked with ghee, *ajaji* (cumin) and *samudra* salt (sea salt) over a charcoal fire, each of these being added in succession while the meat is cooking over a gridiron.

पिशितं सौरभैर्लिप्तं कन्दुपक्वम् मधुप्रभम् ।
राजिकाकल्कलिप्तं च कन्दुपाचितमुच्यते ।

Sushruta says meat cooked with sesame or mustard paste and with condiments to a honey colour in a tandoor is called *Kandu Pakvam*.

सिक्त्वा सिक्त्वाम्बुधाराभिः विधूमेऽग्नौ प्रतापयेत् ।
फलाम्लेनापि यत्पक्वं शल्यं तत्सौरभान्वितम् ।

Here Sushruta also mentions another meat preparation called *Shulyam*, for which the meat has to be soaked in asafoetida water and cooked over a gridiron on a smokeless fire. During cooking, a mixture of water and pomegranate juice is sprinkled over the meat.

Stein, the great archaeologist, while at work in a place called Lou-Lon along the Silk Route, discovered manuscripts written in an ancient Indian script. They revealed the final outpost of the Indian Empire. Traders, mostly from Punjab, travelling on this route, had left behind food habits as far as Lou-Lon. In his own words Stein describes this as his most thrilling discovery. Till then no one had any knowledge of how far the Indian trading community had spread during the rule of the Kushan kings. All the earlier history had come to us in the form of coins and a few copper plates made at various times during their rule. Now here was proof of their grandeur. People enjoyed good food! Indian religious, political and cultural influence spread from Afghanistan to Western and Central Asia, up to Chinese Turkistan. The caravans of traders travelling to these parts from India carried their tandoors with them. With so many people to feed, the womenfolk always had their hands full. In the afternoons, when the caravans halted, the tandoors were lighted. In a jiffy everyone had bread (roti) to eat! The following day, breakfast was of *navala* — stale bread.

With the decline of the Kushan Empire, trade declined. The difference between 'Shah' and 'Gumashta', as the saying goes, disappeared. The traders became a part of the local populace. But they still savoured the taste of food eaten in earlier years. And so it was that while all other traditions were forgotten, the fire under the tandoor was still lit in the homes of these traders-turned-settlers.

Buddhist culture then gradually gained popularity. Being vegetarian, the emphasis shifted to baking breads. The diet consisted of wheat, rice, pulses, vegetables, milk and milk products. Meat was eaten mostly by the warrior classes or some low caste people.

During the Gupta period that followed around AD 320–540, the best of both the Buddhist and the Hindu traditions were revived. Peace and prosperity prevailed, great literature was written and traditional values upheld.

With the advent of the power of Islam, Kabul and Ghazni were occupied by Turks. The local population converted to Islam. In AD 711 Mohammad Bin Kassim annexed Sindh upto Multan, a great centre for trade and industry at that time. There was no central power in northern India at this time, and no major invasion took place between AD 711 and 1175.

Prosperity led to decadence in every sphere of life. Moral values declined and the effects were visible in the arts and literature. Fortunately, food gained prominence. The art of cooking became more elaborate. Simplicity gave way to complexity. Food was presented in many more varieties, using more spices, ingredients, colours and decorations.

As a part of our heritage we have the first 'cookery book' that gives us this information. *Manasollasa,* which literally means 'joy fulfilment' was written by Somesvara in AD 1127. It details many methods of cooking, dealing specially with food habits of the aristocracy. Both vegetarian and non-vegetarian kitchens have been described in depth.

Around AD 1175 Mohammad Ghori captured Multan, Kutch and Sindh from the Arabs, and also annexed Punjab from the Ghaznavi lineage. During a period of continuous change, Delhi saw a succession of dynasties including the Slave Kings, Khiljis, Tughlaqs, Sayyads and the Lodis.

During this time, AD 1200–1500, conditions in Punjab were quite unstable. People were tyrannised by the local jagirdars — the governors' representatives. Only those who had access to royalty could maintain large kitchens!

It was in these troubled times that Guru Nanak (AD 1469–1539) founded a new religion in Punjab called Sikhism. His teachings greatly impressed people. His thoughts and words were simple, he preached against superstition, idol worship, the caste system, and the hypocrisy of the priests, amongst other things. An important step he took was to bring all people together under the concept of *langar*. Here, people of all castes sat and ate together. The tandoor was used to its full potential and was able to serve hot, freshly baked bread to many people at a time. The Guru urged people to have common tandoors in their lanes. This not only did away with the concept of high and low caste, it was a great fuel saver. The *sanjha chulha* or common oven as it was called, proved

Panch pyare at a langar

extremely popular with the womenfolk. It was economical and gave them a common platform to exchange ideas and daily news.

The concept took root quickly and spread all over Punjab and the North-West Frontier Provinces. In many places, the tandoor was lit for all to bake their bread. People of every tone came — caste, creed and colour were forgotten. The goal was common: to bake fresh bread for the hungry stomach.

I wish the tandoor could inculcate such values today.

In AD 1526, Babar invaded India. Descended from the great lineage of Timur and Chenghiz Khan, he fought many battles to establish the Mughal empire in India, which was to be consolidated by Humayun and Akbar. It is from Akbar's time that we really get an insight into the eating habits of the Mughal emperors. It is said the *Badshah* had a large number of employees to attend to different departments of the kitchen. Many kinds of breads were made in various shapes and sizes as described in the *Ain-i-Akbari*. One type of bread was baked in the tandoor, and another type on skillets.

By this time every major town had a *nanbai* in the bazar — a baker selling a variety of breads, freshly baked in the tandoor!

Writings during Emperor Shah Jahan's rule describe three new kinds of breads, one of which was called *roghni*. Made from fine flour and clarified butter, this was baked in the tandoor. It came out as thin leaves and there were two varieties, salty and sweet.

In *Travels in the Mughal Empire* written during Aurangzeb's time, Francoise Bernier, while describing the march of the Emperor from Delhi to Kashmir, says that as rotis sold in the bazars were not fit to be eaten, the kings and noblemen invented metallic tandoors that were carried on camel back, to give them good, hot, freshly baked bread.

With the Mughal empire in its ascendancy, prosperity ensured good living. The rich had large kitchens and food was important. Even when the Mughal empire started to disintegrate, food habits remained, and the *nawabs* carried on eating, wining and dining as before.

In *Lakhnavi ka Dastarkhan*, a work in Urdu, the writer says that the tandoor was the popular oven to bake breads. Each noble had specialist cooks to prepare these breads. New breads evolved — plain breads, leavened breads, sweet breads as well as stuffed breads.

A nobleman by the name of Mirza Zaffar Hussain had a bread made in unbelievable proportions: the dough consisted of 20 kg of flour and 20 kg of clarified butter. Can you imagine that!

By now the tandoor was an integral part of the North Indian kitchen. The subjection of the Mughals to British rule did little to change this. The tandoor held its own just as it had done down the ages. During the Second World War one could get delicious mince-meat seekh kebabs made in the tandoor at Nisbat Road in Lahore. In the frontier areas and Punjab, preparations of meat and fowl like *teetar, bater,* chicken, all made in the tandoor, were popular.

Independence caused great upheavals, displacing many. Luckily, food habits endured. Moti Mahal, the famous tandoori food restaurant in Delhi started by one such pioneering family from the frontier, gained tremendous popularity, as have others established since. Over the years the cuisine has acquired 'five-star' status, with one of the most popular restaurants serving tandoori food being Bukhara at the Welcomgroup Maurya Sheraton in New Delhi. Started by Madan Jaiswal, a chef with a great wealth of knowledge and expertise on the tradition of tandoori cooking, this restaurant was one of the first of its kind.

Tandoori chicken and roti are now world famous. When one stops to think that the appliance we have today is a form of what primitive man might have used, the historical ethos of the tandoor becomes quite amazing. I have tried to trace the enduring, over 5000 year history of the tandoor, so that, realizing how old the tradition is, you will look at and enjoy the recipes here with new respect and affection.

Bukhara, Welcomgroup Maurya Sheraton, New Delhi

Construction site, Tees Hazari, Delhi, India

Construction of
the Tandoor

The tandoor works on the same principle as the oven. However, it is the only kind of oven that provides complete wrap-around heat, whether by accident or design. No modern oven has that capability, making the tandoor one of the most scientific and versatile of all cooking apparatus. By controlling the draught and quality of fuel, we are able to produce temperatures upto 400°C. It can be built on site from good clay and uses chopped, dry timber as fuel. Counter sunk and mud plastered, it can be ready for heating in three days. If built of clay, however, it needs six to seven days to dry. The fact remains that you do not have to go anywhere special to make a tandoor, and you can make one wherever you are.

There is one intriguing question: why was it the Asians made and used this apparatus? The answer takes us back to some basic rituals. It was the Hindus and Zoroastrians who held fire in great reverence, and knew how to produce it, fire being the most important energy source for this magnificent apparatus. Once heating was available, tandoori cooking was set in action.

Tandoors are constructed for two kinds of use: the simple tandoor for home use, and the larger professional tandoor to provide greater quantity and longer cooking hours. Making a tandoor is a skilled art more commonly found amongst the people of Punjab who migrated to other parts of the country, and it remains very much a part of their heritage today. In Delhi, one of the most popular places to get a tandoor, or to be able to see one being constructed, is the old Sabji Mandi area between Tees Hazari Courts and Chowk Barafkhana.

The most famous (well-known) tandoor maker in Delhi goes by the name of Munni Lal. His family has been in the trade of constructing tandoors for three generations. With tandoori food becoming so popular, he has been making and setting up tandoors all over the world. A visit to his factory is a fascinating experience, as can be seen from the visuals shot there—a blend of traditional art with modern techniques.

Materials and Preparation

The basic material required for constructing a tandoor is clay, which is free of any sand content. A non-pliable substance like *munj,* a kind of grass, is mixed with this clay, along with other natural binders. Highly plastic clay should be avoided, for while it is convenient to work with, this type of clay usually develops cracks after drying.

The clay is prepared by beating it with the hands and then kneading it. It may also be beaten with a simple, flat, broad piece of wood or stone. Binders are then added with water. The mixture is kneaded with hands or feet, covered with a sack and kept wet for three or four days.

The next stage involves the shaping of the clay which is also done by hand. The tandoor is generally put together in sections. There are two methods of making the tandoor: the more common 'modelling' technique and the not so common 'coiling' technique.

The Modelling Method

Stage I: Once the clay is ready for use, slabs about
12–15 cms wide, 50–60 cms long and 2–3 cms thick, are
made. Some dry clay is sieved on to these and then they are
rolled into cylinders. These cylinders are then unrolled into a
sort of semi-circle. Two or three such unrolled cylinders are
moulded together into a circle. This circle forms the base of
the tandoor.

Stage II : After the base is made, the uppermost part of this
ring is pinched at intervals to create little notches. It is then
left to dry overnight so that it becomes hard and ready to
receive the weight of the next ring.

Stage III : When the clay has dried to the correct hardness, another ring is fused on top of this ring. This smooth and wet clay ring fits on top of the earlier ring, especially where the notches have been pinched. This is designed to give the tandoor firmness and stability. Subsequent sections are then added until the required height is reached.

Stage IV : This involves the shaping of the last section on top, which is turned inwards by hand and shaped like the upper part of a pitcher.

The tandoor is now complete.

The Coiling Method

As the name suggests this method uses clay rolled into a long rope that is coiled upon itself very carefully until the required height is reached. The top of the tandoor is shaped in the same way as the rest. The sides are smoothened with the hand. The finished tandoor should show no sign of ridges. After the tandoors are ready, they are left out to dry.

Later an opening of about 10 cms is made at the bottom to allow circulation of air. This is, of course, essential for temperature control as well as the removal of ashes.

Curing

A certain amount of curing is necessary before the tandoor is fired for the first time. A good new tandoor should be smooth from the inside. Green leaves, usually spinach, are used to coat the inside walls. After a day, a mixture of buttermilk or *khatti lassi*, oil, and salt is rubbed all over the inner walls and left overnight. This curing prevents the rotis and other breads from sticking to the walls of the tandoor when being cooked.

An expert's tip—a coating of molasses will serve the purpose just as well as the above ingredients.

After curing, the tandoor should be lit on low heat on the first and second day for a short duration of about half an hour each day. On the third day it is ready to be used. To keep your tandoor in good order, coat the inner walls with the paste of greens or molasses at least once a fortnight.

Fuel

From the time that Kalibangan revealed the tandoor to us, we have known that wood was the fuel originally used for firing the tandoor. Today, in the simpler home environment or in other non-professional settings, wood is still used as fuel for the tandoor. It should be non-resinous and the fire non-smoky. Once the wood has burnt to charcoal and has fully heated the walls of the tandoor, these become free of soot and ready for use. These days charcoal is the shortcut, convenience fuel. Coke is never used as it has a certain sulphur content, and is not good for cooking.

Twigs of aromatic herbs are added to the fuel during cooking. This gives the dish being cooked a wonderful fragrance and flavour. Charcoal wood itself imparts a special flavour: a good example of this is tandoori chicken — imbued with the smoky taste of fat falling on hot charcoal!

The home tandoor takes just twenty to forty minutes to heat up. The larger professional tandoor takes two to three hours to heat up and operates for about six to eight hours at a time.

If one were to carry out an evaluation with modern technical instruments, one would have to come to the conclusion that there is not much that can be done to improve this cooking appliance.

The home clay tandoor in use, New Delhi, India

Tandoor the World Over

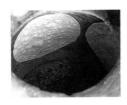

In India we have basically two types of tandoors. The small home tandoor and the larger, commercial tandoor. The home clay tandoor is small in size and can accommodate eight to ten rotis at a time. The last few years have seen a major change in the home tandoor. In a major improvisation, the tandoor is now enclosed in a metallic drum. This prevents it from cracking and it can be carried from place to place. Sizes vary from the littlest ones with a capacity of six to eight rotis to the largest ones that can bake twenty to twenty-five rotis at a time.

The commercial tandoor is usually a much larger version that has been enclosed in brick walls that have been cemented. The gaps between the cement-plastered walls and the tandoor are filled with sand. Sand is a good conductor of heat and also serves as the heat bank. When fixing the tandoor, the mouth of the tandoor should be nearest to where the cook stands, and the opening at the bottom on the left side wall, away from the cook, so that direct heat is not felt while cooking. The counter top is used for holding the basic cooking materials such as dough, flour and water.

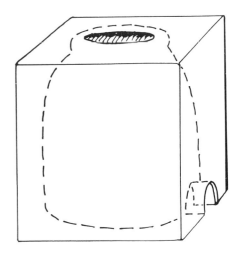

A variation of the traditional clay tandoor, a metallic tandoor made of a special iron-alloy sheet and introduced on an experimental basis, has also proved to be a great success. Its basic construction and proportions are the same. Sizes can vary according to requirement and it bakes just as well as the mud tandoor. The main difference is that this tandoor works on the principle of 'hot air circulation', and the fuel used is cooking gas.

The original gas tandoor designed and developed by Mohley & Mohley

In undivided India, the tandoor was extensively used in the North. Even today, in Baluchistan, the North Western Frontier Province and the Punjab, a variety of tandoors can be seen. Baked terracotta tandoors are usually used in the remote villages of Punjab on festive occasions. These are cylindrical storage jars sunk into the ground and converted into tandoors. Fuel is put in from the top. A side channel replaces the opening at the bottom that allows both air to circulate, and the ashes to be removed. The cooking is done in the usual way, by slapping the dough along the sides of the walls.

Also to be seen are large converted tandoors with tops big enough for men to sit and roll out the dough on, and to be able to put the dough in.

Smaller tandoors, constructed to suit each individual environment, are found in almost every home, and the women are expert bakers of bread.

Punjab, Pakistan

New Delhi, India

Men making rotis for sale, Delhi, India

Roghni nans for sale, Pakistan

Nans for servants at a private house, Baluchistan, Pakistan

Afghani nans for sale in the North-West Frontier Provinces, Pakistan

Afghanistan

Typical of Afghanistan is a very large tandoori nan shown here being made by the Pashtun women for their families which usually consist of twenty or more members. Food here is usually very simple. Nan and lentils or vegetable. Only for special occasions do they cook meat in the form of a pullao and a variety of five to six vegetables.

57

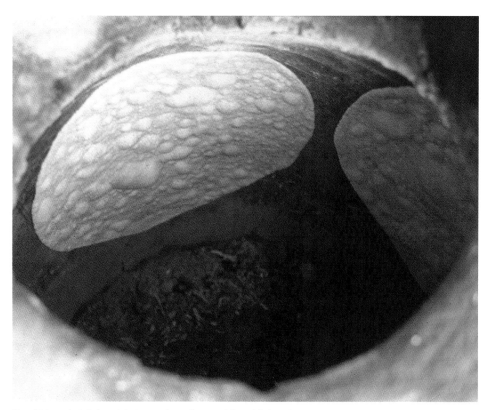

Traditional step by step procedure for making Afghani nan

Afghanistan

Egypt

In Egypt, the men bake bread in the sand within twenty minutes. This is eaten with a single dish of meat or vegetables. Unmarried girls, who are allowed to take the goats to pasture, also do the same for their midday meal. Bread and tea make up their lunch.

China

China is also familiar with the tandoor. In North China, a very special dish called the Peking Duck is still prepared in the tandoor. This dish, as served at the more sophisticated restaurants in other parts of the world, is usually cooked in the oven.

The tandoors in China were made with a very special porcelain clay that is specific to that region. The basic construction and operation is the same, the only difference being that this tandoor has a lid. To cook the Peking Duck skewers are replaced with hooks.

Iran

Known as a *tanoor*, the tandoor is, even today, extensively used in Iran to bake nans. No one makes these at home, for they are available as is our bread, at every corner in each locality. The three main types are called *berbery, sangak* and *lavash.*

The tandoors are very big, with a floor made of brick or stone. The dough is rolled out by an assistant and put on a board that has a long stick attached to it. The *nanva,* as he is known, puts this board through the small opening of the tandoor and the dough goes on the floor. Thirty to forty nans can be had in one heating. The nan baked on a brick floor is the berbery and is generally eaten at breakfast. It is slightly thick and oval shaped. The top is patterned with the fingers. The nan baked on a stone floor is called sangak. This nan has the impression of the stones on it, is crisp and delicious, and is generally eaten at the midday meal.

Lavash is made in a mud tandoor similar to those we have in India though bigger in size. It is slapped on to the sides with the help of a pad and picked up as it cooks. It is very thin and keeps well for a number of days.

Arab Countries

Some desert tribes still use a very primitive form of the tandoor that can be constructed at any site where clay and twigs are available. Once ready, twigs and leaves are burnt in this oven and when it is hot, the flattened dough is stuck onto the sides. When baked, it falls off and is taken out. Sometimes a stand is constructed in the middle of the tandoor on which a single pot of meat curry or dal is cooked along with the breads being prepared.

Caucasus

In the Caucasian region, an oven called *tone* resembles the tandoor and also works on the same principle. It is made from bricks and measures three feet across and four feet in depth. The dough is usually patted into an elongated shape, placed in the tone and baked till it is golden brown.

Europe

By a strange coincidence, during one of my visits to Zurich while writing this text, I came across a traditional clay cooking pot called the *romertopf* in the home of my friends Margrith and Shubusen Gupta.

Trying out a tandoori recipe for chicken tikka, I found that this little dish can serve as a makeshift tandoor. One has to, of course, put the dish in the oven. As the romertopf heats up, it imparts a wrap-around heat similar to that in a tandoor. The skewers resting on the edges of the dish have to be turned occasionally, the drippings falling to the bottom of the dish. Following the traditional method of basting the meat a couple of times, we can get an authentic tasting tandoori dish in about thirty-five to forty minutes.

Malai chicken tikka being made in a romertopf

Part
II

Invisible Work
Before Cooking

*A great deal of invisible or preparatory work
takes place in tandoori cooking,
particularly with meats.
Sometimes these stages have to be completed
almost a day before the dish is to be served.*

*They usually consist of washing with
natural deodorizers, and one to three marinades,
which have integrated tenderizers in them
and spices for flavour.*

*Since there is no time to 'resolve' meats
during cooking in a tandoor or
for that matter on a spit or European grill,
the meats have to be tenderized first.*

*After this the meat only needs to be singed
or cooked in the tandoor,
usually a matter of five to twenty minutes at most,
depending on the type of meat used.*

*The recipes appear to take up so much space
because of the need to describe these stages,
which have been codified for convenience.
At the end basting is done with specified fat,
mostly ghee or oil, and some leftover marinade.
Ghee is by far the best
as it does not 'burn' at high temperatures.
One should not, therefore, be
intimidated by the length of the recipe, nor
daunted by the time and tedium
involved in preparing the meats
for the tandoor.*

*Most consumers only see the skewers
actually put inside the tandoor
and, lo and behold, you are served before
you may be ready to eat!*

The point to appreciate is that
without tenderizing and marination,
the meats will never cook properly
or taste so good.
It is in tenderizing, using
spices and their impregnation,
that the secret
of really good tandoori meat lies.
To achieve this, you have to
work six to eight hours before cooking.

All that you have prepared and kept ready
in accordance with the various stages,
and in the quantities required,
is perfected in the tandoor within minutes.
The impact of tandoori food
when served is spectacular.

Butter being churned by hand in an earthen pot. Traditionally ghee was made
at home by clarifying butter.

Basic Preparation

Every cuisine uses certain preparations that are special to its place of origin. These impart their own unique flavour and aroma to the dish served and give it authenticity. In this chapter, I have given the recipes for certain basic, very important preparations and masalas that are best made at home. In fact, it may even be necessary to do so because in many parts of the world these may not be commercially available or of the required quality.

Masalas are the essence of all good cooking. The purer the masala, the tastier the dish. For this one should try to grind spices fresh at home. Always buy the best quality whole spices to get good results. There are two groups of spices. One group of the garam masala spices that can be sun-dried, ground and stored. The other group includes coriander, fenugreek, cumin, caraway, etc, which store better once they are roasted and ground.

When using whole spices to make any masalas, it is better to pound them a bit. They can then be ground in an ordinary or a coffee grinder. Grind once, then sift through a fine sieve. The coarse residue left in the sieve can be ground again. The prepared masala should be transferred into dark, air-tight glass containers, and stored in a cool place. Light, heat and damp destroy much of the quality of a good masala.

Ghee

Ghee, (colloquialized from the Sanskrit *'grith'*) is the purest form of butter fat with practically no milk solids. In this form it is solid and can be stored indefinitely. It has been prepared in India from time immemorial and has been described in ancient texts.

शुचि घृतम् न तप्तमध्यायाः

Rig Veda. 4.1.6.

Butter was heated before use with a view to clarifying it.

At a time when there was no mechanization or refrigeration, cow, buffalo, and in some regions even yak and goat milk was converted to butter using either a curd or a cream intermediary. This was done manually, with ceramic or wooden implements.

Ghee resembles olive oil in that it is without impurities. Besides, it is an excellent cooking medium because it does not change colour under heat and can be re-heated and re-used many times without any change in its characteristics.

For the developing countries, ghee has become very expensive and vegetable oils are being used as an alternative. However, with the surplus of butter in many developed nations, butter-oil has come to be produced and used extensively. Butter-oil, because of its hi-tech processing, tends to lose the original flavour of ghee, but is technically the same product. If you cannot buy ghee or make it, use any cooking oil as recommended in the recipes.

Where butter is cheap and available in plenty, ghee can be made at home. Most cooks in India use no other cooking medium except ghee, specially for red meats.

Preparation and cooking **1 hour**

Double cream	500 g
Cold water	1 cup
Ice cubes*	8-10

Put the double cream in a blender with a whipping attachment. Whip while adding water. The butter will separate from the liquid. In case there seems to be incomplete separation, ice cubes may be added to help the butter solidify. Remove the butter and put it in a heavy-bottomed pan. Heat on a slow fire till the water evaporates and solids precipitate (but not till they are burnt). The remaining liquid is pure ghee.

Dahi (Yoghurt or Curd)

Yoghurt has a fascinating history of its own. It originated in India and was taken to the West by the nomadic tribes and gypsies of Eastern and Central Europe via Asia Minor. It is probable that milk, a staple food for all nomads, when stored, set due to the activity of the ever-present lactobacillus and became accepted as a separate food item.

Yoghurt lends itself to conversion to cheese or butter and is extensively used in Indian kitchens as a meat tenderizer and a sour creaming agent.

It is also eaten with sugar, jam, flavoured with salt condiments, and made into buttermilk. Today it is being added to practically anything: crackers,

* Generally used in hot climates

Curd being sold, Delhi, India

potato wafers, cheese, soups, flans, salad-dressings, toppings, savoury dishes, goulash, stroganoff, etc.

Yoghurt is one of the most nutritious foods and is a complete diet in itself. Besides, it restores the intestinal flora following an imbalance caused by antibiotic therapy.

In case it is not possible to prepare yoghurt at home, buy some cultured yoghurt. If that too is not available, use factory yoghurt.

As yoghurt is a product of bacterial activity, to make yoghurt at home, you have to have a 'starter'. This can initially be taken from cultured yoghurt bought in the market and subsequently put aside from the yoghurt prepared everyday.

Preparation 4 **hours**

| Milk | 3 cups |
| Yoghurt culture | 1 tbsp |

Warm the milk. If the climate is cold, the milk has to be fairly hot. If the climate is warm, the milk should be lukewarm. Take a tablespoon full of culture, spread it evenly in the dish in which you plan to set the yoghurt. Now pour the milk into this dish. Stir well to mix the culture.

There are alternate methods to stirring. One can use a hand whisk, or give the milk with the culture one spin in the blender.

Now set the milk aside for three to four hours to set. In cooler climates, it could take longer, about seven to eight hours, and to ensure that the milk does not cool while setting, it should be covered with a warm cloth or tea-cozy. You can refrigerate the yoghurt after it is set and it can be kept in the refrigerator for a number of days. Even when it sours, it can be used as a tenderizer.

Bandi Dahi
(Hung-Drained Yoghurt)

Literally yoghurt that has been tied up, bandi dahi imparts a unique texture to meats. It has been used in this way to exploit it to its full potential in some of the recipes.

Preparation 4 hours

Yoghurt	2 cups
Muslin cloth	

The preparation is very simple. Tie the yoghurt in a muslin cloth and hang it up. Put a bowl underneath to catch the dripping whey. This is the water that drains out. What is left in the cloth is very close to the European cream cheese, and is what we call hung yoghurt or 'bandhi dahi'. Sometimes the drained water can be added to the sauce to be served with kababs.

Panir

Panir is cottage cheese, and might have originated in India or in Southern Italy where it is called 'ricotta'. The English refer to panir as the Indian cream cheese, though this is not really appropriate as it is closer to ricotta and also perhaps to the Japanese bean curd or 'tofu'.

Panir is very refreshing, neutral, spongy, and has a healthy content of protein and fat. It makes a delectable salad both with and without a dressing. Though available in the market, it is best prepared at home and takes very little time to prepare.

Preparation 1/2 hour

Full cream milk	2 kg
Double cream	3 tbsp
Yoghurt	1/4 cup
Lemon medium	1

Heat the milk till it boils. Add the double cream and stir well. When it boils again add the yoghurt and the juice of a lemon. Stir. When the milk curdles and the water separates from the casein, take a muslin cloth or a cheese cloth, put it over a collander and allow to strain for about half an hour. Panir is what is left behind in the cloth. Do not use a mould or a weight to drain the water. This makes the panir loose.

To make soft-set panir, fold over the muslin cloth to give the panir a cube formation. Place under a light weight for one hour.

To make the panir well-set, put a heavier weight on it and let the weight stay for a couple of hours. Then unwrap and cut to any shape you like — diced, diamond-cut, julienne-cut or square.

For panir tikka, the pressed panir is cut into large square pieces and used.

Tofu

Tofu, as it is called in Japanese, is actually soya bean curd. Its texture resembles panir, and its preparation is also somewhat similar. But its nutritive value is what amazes people. Tofu is very high in protein, vitamins and minerals and low in calories, saturated fats and cholesterol. In other words, the ideal food! I love to cook tofu as it is very versatile and adapts well to all kitchens.

Preparation 4 ½ hours

Soya bean	3½ cup
Water	8 cups
Epsom salts	2 tbsp

Soak the beans for at least twelve hours. Strain and grind in mixie adding water until milky. Remove and strain through a muslin cloth for consistency, collecting the milky portion in a heavy bottom vessel. Mix epsom salts in 4 tbsp of water. Bring soya bean milk to a boil, switch off the heat, and mix the epsom salt in the soya bean milk. This will curdle the milk. Strain the soya bean curd through a cloth that has been placed in the mould. Press the bean curd and put some weight on it. Remove after a couple of hours. Transfer it gently to a container filled with water and refrigerate. Home-made tofu will stay for at least a week, if the water is changed regularly. In cooking, it can be used in the same way as panir.

Facing page: Freshly-made tofu being set in traditional moulds

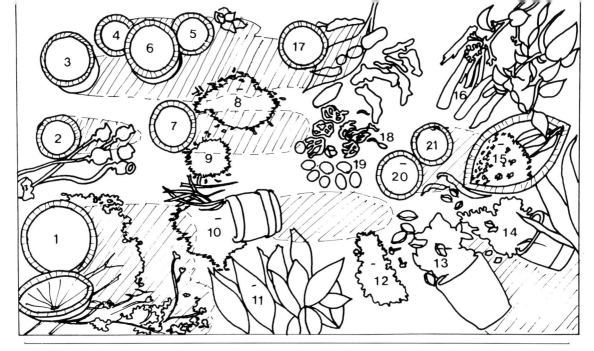

Previous page: 1. Coriander seeds 2. Poppy seeds 3. Black pepper whole 4. White pepper whole
5. Carum seeds 6. Black mustard 7. White mustard 8. Cumin seeds 9. Caraway seeds
10. Fenugreek seeds 11. Bay leaf 12. Clove 13. Brown cardamom 14. Green cardamom
15. Dry red chillies 16. Cinnamon 17. Turmeric 18. Mace 19. Nutmeg 20. Black sesame
seeds 21. White sesame seeds

Garam Masala

Peppercorn	1 tbsp
Caraway	2 tsp
Cumin	1 tbsp
Cardamom green	1½ tbsp
Cardamon brown	1 tsp
Cloves	2 tsp
Cinnamon pieces	½ tbsp
Nutmeg powdered	1 tsp
Mace crushed	1 tsp

Grind all the ingredients together and store.

Aromatic Garam Masala

Cardamom brown	2 tbsp
Cinnamon pieces	2 tbsp
Cloves	2 tbsp

Grind all the ingredients together and store.

Kharasani Ajwain Masala

Another masala that gives a wonderful finishing touch to tandoori dishes.

Cumin	1½ tbsp
Black peppercorn	1½ tbsp
Rock salt	1 tbsp
Carum	1 tsp
Citric acid	1/2 tsp
Raw mango powder	1 tbsp
Dry ginger	1½ tsp
Whole red chillies	2
Vegetable charcoal	3/4 tsp
(Food grade)	

Roast the cumin seeds and red chillies, set aside to cool. Pound the rock salt. Grind the cumin, red chilli and pounded rock salt together. Add all ingredients except vegetable charcoal and grind again. Add the powdered charcoal, mix thoroughly and store.

Tandoori Khatta Masala

The most popular masala eaten with tandoori meats, the khatta masala made according to this recipe is really tasty.

Caraway	1 tsp
Rock salt	1 tbsp
Raw mango powder	2 tsp
Citric Acid	1/4 tsp
Vegetable charcoal	
(Food grade)	1 tsp
Black pepper ground	1 tsp

Pound and grind the rock salt. Roast and grind the caraway seeds. Mix all the ingredients well.

Curry Masala

This masala is usually added to meat when making curries. I have used it for my kababs, adding the finishing touch by sprinkling just a pinch along with a dash of lemon juice to enhance the flavour.

Coriander	6 tbsp
Red chillies	2 tsp
Turmeric powder	3/4 tsp
Cumin	2 tsp
Fenugreek seeds	3/4 tsp
Mustard seeds	3/4 tsp
Black pepper	2 tsp

Roast all the whole spices, mix turmeric and grind well.

Elaichi Jaiphal Masala

This particular masala is always best when freshly made, therefore the quantities given are smaller.

Cardamom green	1 tsp
Cardamom brown	1
Nutmeg grated	1 tsp
Mace	1 tbsp
Black peppercorns	1 tbsp

Powder all ingredients and mix.

Besan Til Masala

Another masala best served fresh.

Whole coriander seeds	2 tsp
Mustard seeds	1/2 tsp
Sesame seeds	1/2 tsp
Compounded asafoetida	
powder	1/4 tsp
Chickpea flour	2 tbsp
Green chillies	4-6
Oil	1 tbsp
Salt	1 tsp

Heat oil in a frying pan. Splutter mustard and coriander seeds. Add the compounded asafoetida powder, then the sesame seeds and stir. Then add the gram flour and salt. Roast well. Turn off the heat, slit the green chillies lengthwise and mix in well with the hot masala. Cover and keep till required.

Fresh and dried kachri

Tenderizers

 It is an interesting fact that cooking in the tandoor used to be limited to breads alone. Except in ancient India, there was relatively little cooking of meat in the tandoor. However, with a knowledge of Indian spices, the most delectable, healthy and quick cooking can be undertaken. And today, meat cooked in the tandoor with the aid of tenderizers specially contributed by India has become the rage the world over.

From what little information is available on the subject, only the stillborn lamb known as *burrah karakul*, from which the karakul fur was obtained, was the meat cooked in the tandoori style. This illustrates the most important factor for cooking meat in the tandoor — only tender meat can be cooked in this way. Cooking heat is limited to temperatures ranging between $200^0 - 400^0C$ and the tandoor cannot contain any vessels for sauting, braising or boiling. Therefore, meats that were not tenderized could not be handled in it.

Borrowing from a famous saying, that 'history was made when the sausage met the mustard' we can say that 'history was remade when meat met the tenderizer'.

Yoghurt set at home

The ancient Indians knew of several tenderizing methods. These were used extensively, and that is why meat cooking in the tandoor is thought to be of Indian origin.

Sushruta Samhita mentions meat being cooked as far back as the fourth century AD. He says meat is naturally energy giving and imparts gloss and strength to the system. Moreover, that which has been cooked and prepared with clarified butter, curd, sour gruel, acid fruits such as the lemon and pomegranate (thereby tenderizing it), pungent and aromatic condiments such as mustard oil, black pepper, etc. (marinades) should be considered a very wholesome diet, being tasty, strength giving and having many tissue building properties.

In spite of this ancient origin, it may astonish many that the best tandoori cooking, with a large variation of meats, came into its own in India only after Partition in 1947. Of course, today the tandoor can be found everywhere, just as tenderizers are available everywhere.

A farmer admiring his mustard crop, Punjab, India

Raw papaya

When meat is tenderized appropriately, it requires only to
be singed at a high temperature — provided by the tandoor.
The essential principles of all tenderizers depend on acid
content and enzymes. These readily dissolve sinews and
muscle fibre, making their use a pleasant necessity. Amongst
tenderizers the most commonly used are yoghurt, raw
papaya, kachri (belonging to the cucumber and melon
family), raw pineapple, and to a limited extent, vinegar.
Often, a number of tenderizers are used together. This is
because the tradition of Indian cooking is not bound by any
restriction or fixed norms. An expert cook can nearly always
modify the taste of the dish to suit the patron.

A brief note on the types of tenderizers used in my recipes, a
general idea on where they are found and in what form they
are used, follows. The tenderizers have been listed in order
of their qualitative importance.

Tenderizers

Raw Pineapple

Raw Figs

Raw Papaya

Raw Mango Powder

Pomegranate Seeds

Tamarind

Curd

Lemon Juice

Mustard Seeds

Yoghurt

Yoghurt was known to ancient Indians long before it became popular anywhere else in the world. It was considered to be a food of high nutritional and religious value.

Basically, yoghurt is fresh milk inoculated with a culture of lactobacillus. It is the lactic acid in yoghurt that helps to break down meat fibres and renders the product soft and succulent when cooked.

With tandoori cooking becoming so popular in most parts of the world, yoghurt has achieved a very high status. It is used in a wide variety of foods, both cooked and uncooked. In curries, it is usually added at the end. In salads it is used as dressing made by draining the extra water content and adding flavouring. In tandoori food it is used as a tenderizer and added at various stages of marination. Yoghurt, in its original form, remains a favourite with me and many of my friends around the world.

Lemon

Indian name: nimbu
Botanical name: *Citrus medica*

Lemons are found in three or four varieties all over India. There is a thin-skinned variety found in upper India, a small, round variety called pati nimbu, and also a large variety called khatta nimbu found in Bengal. The citric acid contained in this fruit is what causes the tenderizing action on the meat fibre. Lemon is used in two ways, for tenderizing and for giving the special finishing touch after the dish is ready.

Raw Papaya

Indian name: papita / papaya
Botanical name: *Carica papaya*

The papaya is an oblong melon-like fruit that grows in most parts of India. The fruit is obtained from a fully grown tree and is used in its raw form. The papaya contains a protein digesting enzyme called papain that gives it its tenderizing property.

Kachri

Indian name: kachri
Botanical name: *Cucumis pubescens*

Kachri is a wild variety of cucumis and is found in Bengal, Punjab, parts of Maharashtra, the North Western Provinces, and the Sind area (now in Pakistan). It is used in its wild form and is seldom cultivated as a crop.

Vinegar

Vinegar is produced when natural yeast in the air acts on the juice of whichever fruit is being used to make the vinegar. It converts the sugar to alcohol, and then this alcohol is converted to acid. Acetic acid is the substance which gives it its tenderizing quality.

The strength of acetic acid in vinegar varies depending on the fruit base. Every country uses vinegar made from locally abundant fruit. Grape and cider vinegars remain the most popular for cooking in the West. Synthetic vinegar is available quite easily and is often used.

Khatti Lassi

This is yoghurt left to ferment and is more acidic than fresh yoghurt. It uses the same principle for tenderizing as yoghurt.

Raw Pineapple

Indian name: ananas
Botanical name: *Ananas sativa*

Most popularly found in Assam and other north-eastern areas, this is an oval, spiky looking fruit with a pungent taste. The active enzyme found in pineapple is bromalein which has a very similar tenderizing action to raw papaya.

Raw Figs

Indian name: anjeer
Botanical name: *Ficus carica*

Figs are found in many parts of India, though mainly the north-west and Punjab. The enzyme which acts as a tenderizer in figs is ficin.

Tamarind

Indian name: imly
Botanical name: *Tamarindus indica*

Found mostly in South India, this is an extremely sour, bean-like fruit with larger seeds. The ripe fruit contains two acids — citric and tartaric — that gives it its characteristic sour taste, and its tenderizing properties.

Brown Mustard

Indian name: rai
Botanical name: *Brassica juncea*

Mustard is found in most parts of India. It is commonly used in the south.

Commercially Prepared Tenderizers

Prepared meat tenderizers are now available in the market. Although a convenient substitute, they can never replace the real thing!

Mechanical Tenderizing

There is one other aspect of tenderizing that needs mention. This is mechanical tenderizing. Often lamb is beaten with a wooden or rubber mallet or scored to facilitate the tenderizing process. This method is used for the preparation of chops, spare ribs, lamb rolls, etc.

Mechanical tenderizing

Marinades

 Marination is a process followed all over the world for food that is to be grilled, barbecued or cooked in the tandoor. The food to be cooked is coated with and left to stand in the marinade for some time. This achieves a dual purpose — it tenderizes and simultaneously spices the food. However, the marinade should only enhance the flavour of what is being cooked, not completely overwhelm the taste of it. All types of meats, game, fowl, pork, beef, fish and a variety of meats including liver and kidney can be marinated.

A marinade consists of tenderizers, herbs, spices and dry fruits. Details of herbs and spices are given in my earlier book *Curry Curry Curry** and we have already discussed tenderizers. In a marinade, we may use a combination of spices, herbs and two or three different types of tenderizers. All marinades are prepared according to the kitchen we are working in. These days, people tend to take short cuts and use commercially prepared tenderizers. Unfortunately, these never give an authentic taste.

While there is no fixed time to allow for marination, the time factor is important and depends on a number of things:

1. The type of meat or fresh vegetable being cooked;
2. The type of cut being used — whole, tikka, or mince;
3. The variety of tenderizers being used.

Prepared meats, tenderized and marinated, can be kept for two to three days in the fridge. You can deep freeze as well for longer storage, but you must then use a microwave for defrosting.

* Penguin 1990

In hot climates, marinated food kept out will spoil. This is because bacterial action takes place at higher temperatures. In such countries it is best to put the dish in the fridge immediately after it has been marinated. The important thing to note is that food should be at room temperature before being put into the tandoor.

Aluminium dishes should never be used to marinate or keep marinated foods. Aluminium imparts an unpleasant metallic taste to the food. Non-metallic and lead-free ceramic dishes are ideal. Stainless steel is also popular today.

The addition of salt during marination needs special mention. For white meats and vegetables, salt can be added together with spices, etc., at the beginning. For red meats, salt should not be added in the first marinade, as the addition of salt releases water and juices from the meat, making it stringy. A certain amount of flavour is also lost. In these meats salt can be added to the marinade fifteen to twenty minutes before cooking.

As always, the modern generation likes quick cooking and short-cuts. For this, there are a number of ready-made spicy salts available in the market. Again, I stress here that these are no substitute for the aroma of freshly ground spices.

Dry fruits are added to impart a distinctive flavour and texture to certain recipes. Sparingly used, they always raise a dish above the ordinary.

Ajwain or carum is a herb with a very distinctive flavour and smell often used in tandoori cooking. The seeds are added in the marinade for vegetables and meats. However, I am totally averse to using it with chicken with which, I feel, it does not blend well.

In summary, a special word of advice: to achieve the best results in tandoori cooking, pay special attention to the essence of marination, for therein lies the secret.

Opposite: Dry fruits for marinades

Basic Marinades

In this era of fast foods people want
quick results. For this I am giving
below three very basic marinades that
can be used for any of the main meats:
chicken, mutton or fish.

For traditional Indian tandoori flavour

Broiler chicken	1 kg
Yoghurt	1 cup
Lemon juice	3 tbsp
Red chillies	1 tsp
Ginger paste	1 tbsp
Garlic paste	2 tsp
Onion paste	3 tbsp
Garam masala	1 tbsp
Cooking oil	1/4 cup
Salt	to taste
Food colour	1 tsp

*Chicken being marinaded for a traditional
Indian tandoori flavour*

Cauliflower florets marinaded for a traditional Indian flavour both with and without food colour

For Chinese flavour

Broiler chicken	1 kg
Vinegar	3/4 cup
Soya sauce	2 tbsp
White wine	2 tbsp
Sesame oil	1 tsp
Cooking oil	1/4 cup
Salt	to taste
Black pepper	2 tsp
Ginger paste	1 tbsp
Garlic paste	2 tsp

For Western flavour

Broiler chicken	1 kg
Vinegar	1/2 cup
Lemon juice	1 tbsp
White wine	1 tbsp
Olive oil	3 tbsp
Salt	to taste
Pepper	1 tsp
Aromatic herbs/spices	to taste
Worcester sauce	1 tbsp

These basic marinades are flexible and a good cook can always make adjustments. All the herbs should be dry ground and mixed with the liquid part of the marinade. The marinade can be stored in a refrigerator for upto a week and can be re-used.

For leaf-wrapping kababs, banana or cabbage leaves are used

The Final Stage

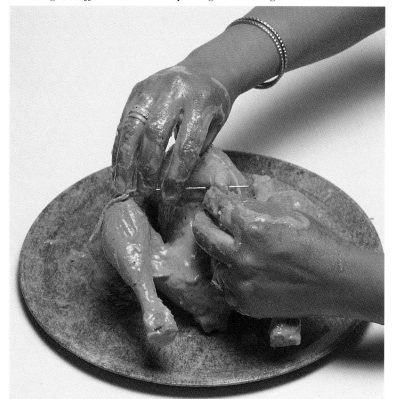

Last, but not least, is the method employed before putting the food in the tandoor. These techniques are compiled from tips and the silent observation of master cooks at work in various kitchens, specially the Oudh, Hyderabadi and Rampur kitchens. I feel that, after reading all the special points in this text, a novice could well become an authority.

Stitching a stuffed chicken. Recipe: Vegetable Murg Mussallam

Seekh

According to me the seekhs or skewers are the skeletons supporting the system. They play a very important part in this cuisine. Made from wrought iron, they absorb and conduct heat, cooking the meat both from the inside and outside.

The seekhs should always be greased and rubbed with a cloth before putting anything on them. I have stressed this point in every recipe.

Different seekhs serve different purposes. They are generally about one centimetre thick, round, and vary in length, depending on the size of the tandoor. I prefer round seekhs. The meat does not slip off as some people believe, the technique of skewering being of prime importance.

Mince kabab seekhs are pointed at both ends. This enables a seekh with a number of kababs to be cooked from both ends and for the kababs to be removed from either side.

It is important to know that delicate meats like fish, prawns and vegetables need thinner seekhs, as larger seekhs tend to break open the meat or vegetable being cooked.

Bread seekhs come in pairs. One is bent at a right angle about an inch from the end. The other ends in a small spatula. When the bread is ready it is caught with the hooked skewer and supported from the back with the spatula end of the skewer. In case the bread is still sticking to the walls of the tandoor when it is ready, a gentle scraping is done with the help of this skewer to take it off.

Different kinds of seekhs. From left to right: round, square and a pair of bread seekhs. Above them is the bread cushion.

One special accessory needed for making breads in the tandoor is a kind of cushion, usually stuffed with coconut coir. The prepared dough is placed on this cushion and then slapped on to the side walls, the basic idea being one of providing support in the process of 'slapping on'. The bigger the bread the larger the cushion. A couple of clean dusters can be tied around a wad of coir to make this.

Hooks

For stuffed chicken and leaf-wrapped dishes we can make use of the hook, one hook linked to another, rather like a chain, to get the required length. This chain is then suspended in the tandoor, with the support of a seekh resting across the lips of the upper opening.

Where skewering is difficult, as in the case of the leaf-wrapped kabab, hooks can be used for suspension in the tandoor.

Stitching and Tying

When a recipe makes use of a whole stuffed chicken, it has to be stitched up before being suspended in the tandoor. The stitching is done from the same end from where the insides of the chicken have been cleaned. A trussing needle and kitchen thread can be used for this exercise. Button-holing the thread will ensure that the stitching does not open.

Whole stuffed vegetables have to be tied well before skewering. I have found that inserting tooth-picks at opposite ends to hold the thread while it is being wrapped around is very successful.

A stuffed brinjal tied before it is skewered

97

Skewering

It is important to skewer the meat being cooked in the correct manner. For this we should take into account one or two things. The pieces of flesh should never be arranged end to end. Some gap should be left in between as well as at both ends. Ghee or any edible oil should be applied to clean skewers before threading and then wiped.

While threading the meat, the skewers should not be pushed straight through but 'woven' through in an up and down movement. This ensures that the plane of meat fibre is on different levels and there is no chance of the meat slipping off the skewer.

Whole chickens need to be skewered carefully. The skewer should be inserted from the neck end and should come out near the tail. It should pass along the back in an up and down movement, without breaking the backbone.

The ready-threaded skewer should be allowed to stand for about ten to fifteen minutes. This allows the marinade to dry completely. If it is found to be too dry, oil may be applied. Cooking time is usually anywhere between ten to thirty-five minutes, till the aroma from the meat spreads. The skewer should then be taken out and the juices allowed to drip for four to five minutes while the meats are still on the skewer. These half-cooked skewers can be kept upto three or four hours.

In hot climates, however, meat should not be kept half-prepared for more than two hours. When required, the skewers can be put back in the tandoor as per the time indicated in each recipe.

To remove meats from the skewers one can use any of the breads — nan, roti, etc. Hold the meat firmly with these and, with a twisting motion, slip it off the skewer. It is easiest to take meat off while hot. This technique is easily mastered in a couple of attempts.

The finished product requires one final touch that people often overlook — the garnish masala. Here, the basic herb flavour (in its powdered form) that is used in the marinade, is mixed with a souring element (also in powdered form) and salt. This is sprinkled on top and gives the desired distinctive flavour. Details of the garnish masala are given separately with every recipe.

Skewering broccoli and other green vegetables. Recipe: Hari Seekh

An assortment of quick-fix tandoori food awaiting customers, Delhi, India

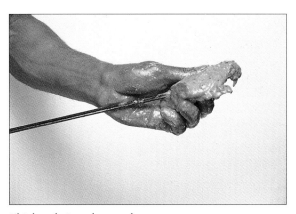

Chicken being skewered

तवत्यं पितो रसा रजांस्यनु विष्ठिताः । दिवि वाता इव श्रिताः

Thy flavours, food are diffused through the regions,
and like winds are spread in the sky.

Rigveda. 1. 187

Part
III

The Recipes

The following section details over seventy traditional and non-traditional recipes. Before you embark on your journey into the tandoor civilization, I would like you to read carefully a couple of points mentioned here.

Where there are no clay tandoors, gas tandoors have successfully been used, though only for a small family. These are available in the Indian market and can be carried by anyone going west who wishes to cook tandoori food.

In the western market the meat is generally softer as it is pre-tenderized specially for prime cuts. All our recipes are suited to the kinds of meat available in India. The marination time should be reduced to half where pre-tenderized meats are used. Tenderizers given in most recipes are commonly found in India. Of course, a lot of these are available in the west as well. In case one is not able to get a particular tenderizer, commercial meat tenderizers may be used and instructions written on the packet followed.

Manual grinding is outdated today, and dry grinding can always be done in a spice grinder. Pastes should be made with as little water as possible. The Indian silbatta works well here.

While preparing seekh kababs with minced meats, ensuring minimum water content is very important, specially when adding the paste of raw papaya, ginger, garlic or onion. It is always better to use the paste of fried onions in seekh kababs. If raw onions are to be used chopped or minced, add a pinch of salt and keep aside for five to ten minutes. Then drain out the water and use. Raw tomatoes should never be added to mince meat kababs.

Every recipe given here contains certain amounts of chilli, colour and salt. The quantities against the ingredients need not be taken as pharmacy measures. In Indian cooking a little more or less will not alter the dish and measures can be changed to suit different palates.

Yoghurt is considered one of the best tenderizers in the Indian kitchen. Fresh yoghurt is what we all use in our homes, but there is an aspect that is sometimes overlooked — the marinade sauce should never be too liquidy. Yoghurt hung for about fifteen minutes has the ideal consistency for the marinade base. In these fifteen minutes all the superfluous water is drained out leaving it perfect for marination.

All the recipes can be cooked in the oven. The basic thumb rule to remember is that it takes a tandoori dish twice as long to cook in an oven. So, double the cooking time and place the marinated meats on a wire rack above a tray to collect the drippings. These can be used for basting along with oil.

Barbecues and spits have also been successfully used for tandoori dishes. The cooking time remains almost the same, though on a spit or barbecue you have to turn the skewers. One must realize that tandoori cooking is not hi-tech; a plus or minus time of about five to ten minutes is always possible, and one should check the dish to one's own satisfaction before serving.

The temperature of the tandoor can be varied by closing or not closing the upper opening and by regulating the draught from the lower opening. Chart No. I indicates how. Chart No. II gives temperatures at which some of the more common dishes are prepared.

Chart No I

1.	Upper and lower open, charcoal burning	380°C
2.	Upper and lower open, charcoal burnt out	350°C
3.	Upper and lower closed for 10 minutes	300°C
4.	Upper open, lower partially closed	250°C
5.	Upper open, lower closed	200°C

Chart No II

Dish Temperatures

1.	Chicken	250°C
2.	Tikka kabab	250°C
3.	Seekh kabab	250°C
4.	Fish	180°C – 200°C
5.	Roti	200°C
6.	Nan	200°C
7.	Paratha	250°C
8.	Cauliflower, panir and other vegetable kababs	200°C

A glossary of English-Indian names and metric weight equivalents is given at the end of the recipe section. All teaspoon and tablespoon measures are level, and the abbreviations used are:

tsp	=	teaspoon
tbsp	=	tablespoon
g	=	grams
kg	=	kilograms

Finally, I would like to say that such sharing of views and ideas, improvisations, improvements and discussion of techniques can go on forever; but if you cook with a big heart the result is always satisfying.

Poultry

Poultry is a very misleading word, as many people associate only chicken with poultry. No doubt, chicken is more universal, but many varieties of birds are eaten all over the world including India of course, chicken is the most popular dish. For where would we be without that delicious aroma of smoky chicken in the tandoor.

Other types of poultry more popular in India include partridge (*teetar*) and quail (*bater*). Turkey, duck, geese, guinea fowl and pigeons are more popular in western countries.

Chicken is white meat, and care should be taken while cooking as it is delicate to handle. There are four basic cuts used in the tandoori kitchen :

Whole chicken	The ideal is a small broiler chicken between 800 – 900 g.
Large pieces	Usually eight in number, four each of the breast and legs.
Tikka	Small, boneless, two inch pieces from the breast and legs.
Mince	This is chicken meat run once through the mincer.

Unless specified, whenever whole chicken is used in the recipes, it is always understood to be without skin. The best results are obtained from broiler chicken, and that is what I have used in the recipes. Buying chicken is no longer a tedious task. Nowadays, just as you can get 'quick-fix' tandoori chicken, you can always buy 'quick-fix' chicken cuts, and the task becomes that much easier.

Green Sabja Chicken

This preparation is quite unique. Besides using normal tenderizers, it is smeared with a paste of greens.

Preparation and marination **6 ½ hours**
Cooking **20 minutes**

Broiler chicken whole	800 g
Marinade	
Yoghurt	1 cup
Raw papaya paste	2 tbsp
Ginger paste	2 tbsp
Garlic paste	1 tbsp
Turmeric powder	1/2 tsp
Coriander powder	1 tbsp
Oil	1/4 cup
Salt	1 tsp
Paste of Greens	
Green capsicum large	1/2
Green chillies deseeded	3
Green spinach chopped	2 cups
Green coriander	1/4 cup
Onion sliced and fried	1/4 cup
Ghee	1/4 cup
Corn flour	2 tbsp
Vinegar	2 tbsp
Salt	1 tsp

Basting
Balance ghee in which
  onions were fried

Garnish masala
Tandoori khatta masala
Cucumber yoghurt salad

Clean the chicken. Make cuts on the breast and legs. Mix all the ingredients of the marinade and rub the mix all over the chicken. Leave aside for one hour.

Soak the spinach in water for fifteen to twenty minutes, then wash thoroughly to remove any grit. Boil for five minutes and drain. Deseed the green capsicum. Make a paste of all the greens including the fried onion, adding the salt, vinegar and corn flour while grinding. Do not use any water; the onion and capsicum provide enough texture for grinding. Rub the paste into the chickens, filling in the cuts well. Leave aside for five hours.

Oil and wipe the skewer. Skewer the chicken. Put the skewer into the tandoor and cook for ten minutes. Remove and stand upright against the tandoor to let the drippings fall for about five minutes. Baste well and put the skewer back into the tandoor for five to seven minutes. When ready, garnish and serve.

Omar Khayyam-ka-Murg

'Here with a Loaf of Bread beneath the Bough,
A Flask of Wine, a Book of Verse, and Thou,
Beside me singing in the Wilderness,
And Wilderness is Paradise enow.'

Preparation and marination **6 hours**
Cooking **25 minutes**

Broiler chicken whole	800 g
Marinade	
Yoghurt	1 cup
Raw papaya paste	1 tbsp
Kachri powder*	2 tsp
Ginger paste	2 tbsp
Garlic paste	1 tbsp
Red chilli powder	2 tsp
Oil	1/4 cup
Salt	1 tsp
Food colour	few drops
Stuffing	
Indian cottage cheese	1/2 cup
Yoghurt hung	1/2 cup
Green chillies	4
Cardamom green ground	4
Ginger grated	1 tsp
Poppyseed	1 tsp
Rose petals	few
Almonds skinned and pounded	1/2 cup
Pistachio pounded	2 tbsp
Sultanas deseeded	2 tbsp
Figs chopped	2 tbsp
Corn flour	2 tbsp
Salt	1 tsp
Basting	
Ghee	1/4 cup
Garnish	
Mixed vegetable pickle	
Green mint chutney	

Clean the chicken. Make cuts on the breast and legs. Mix all ingredients of the marinade and rub the mix all over the chicken. Leave aside for five hours.

Make fresh panir and hung yoghurt. Mix with all the other ingredients for the stuffing and stuff the marinated chicken. Stitch** the chicken. Coat with any leftover marinade.

Suspend on a hook and chain arrangement and cook in the tandoor for ten minutes. Remove and leave the chicken suspended to let the drippings fall for about five minutes. Baste and put it back into the tandoor for ten minutes. When ready, garnish and serve.

* See glossary of names. Commercial tenderizers may be substituted wherever tenderizing ingredients like kachri or raw papaya are not available.
** See The Final Stage

Facing page: Vegetable Murg Mussallam.
Recipe overleaf.

Stuffing and stitching the marinated chicken

Vegetable Murg Mussallam

This dish is so wholesome, when cooking it you don't have to plan a larger menu. Serve it with tandoori paratha and yoghurt salad, the whole family will enjoy it.

Preparation and marination **7 hours**
Cooking **25 minutes**

Broiler chicken whole	900 g
Marinade	
Yoghurt	1 cup
Lemon juice	2 tbsp
Garam masala	1 tsp
Ginger paste	2 tbsp
Garlic paste	1 tbsp
Red chilli powder	2 tsp
Oil	1/4 cup
Salt	1 tsp
Stuffing	
Peas shelled	1/4 cup
Potatoes diced	1/4 cup
Carrot diced	3 tbsp
Tomato medium chopped	1
Onion large sliced	1
Raw mango powder	1 tsp
Green chillies chopped	2
Green coriander chopped	1/4 cup
Ginger slivered	1 tbsp
Ghee	2 tbsp
Salt	1 tsp
Basting	
Oil	1/4 cup
Garnish	
Raw mango powder	
Any yoghurt salad or relish	

Clean the chicken. Make cuts on the breast and legs. Mix all the ingredients of the marinade and rub the mix all over the chicken. Leave aside for six hours. To make the stuffing proceed as follows:

Heat the basting oil and deep fry the onion, remove and keep aside. Heat the ghee and add all the stuffing ingredients except the fried onions. Cook on a low flame till the vegetables are three-quarters done. Cool the mix, crush and add onions. Stuff and stitch the marinated chicken.

Suspend on a hook and chain arrangement and cook in the tandoor for ten minutes. Remove and leave the chicken suspended to let the drippings fall for about five minutes. Baste and put it back into the tandoor for ten minutes. When ready, garnish and serve.

Golden Chargha Chicken

This is an unusual and delicious chicken recipe with golden crisp skin.

Preparation and marination **8 hours**
Cooking **40 minutes**

Broiler chicken with skin	800 g
Marinade 1	
Lemon juice	1/4 cup
Garlic paste	1 tsp
Red chilli powder	2 tsp
Oil	1/4 cup
Marinade 2	
Yoghurt	1 cup
Oil	3 tbsp
Onions large sliced	2
Ginger paste	2 tbsp
Onion paste	1/4 cup
Cumin powder	1 tsp
Cinnamon piece ground	1/4 tsp
Cloves ground	2
Cardamom green ground	6
Black peppercorns ground	10
Salt	1 tsp
Stuffing	
Onions quartered	3
Ginger chopped	1 tsp
Garlic chopped	1 tsp
Cloves powdered	1/2 tsp
Green chillies chopped	3
Salt	a pinch
Basting	
Honey	1/2 cup
Ghee	1/4 cup

Garnish

Garam masala
Rock salt powdered
Lemon juice
Chilli garlic chutney

Clean the chicken. Draw back the skin from the chicken in various places, make cuts in the breast and legs. Mix all the ingredients of Marinade 1, rub the mix into it. Cover again with the skin. Leave aside for one hour.

In the meantime fry the onions in the basting ghee till they are brown and crisp. Take them out and crush nicely. Mix these with all the other ingredients of Marinade 2 and rub all over, as well as inside, the chicken. Leave aside for six hours. Mix ingredients for stuffing with Marinade 2 left in the dish and pack into chicken. Stitch it up well.

Suspend on a hook and chain arrangement and cook in the tandoor for ten minutes. Remove and leave the chicken suspended to let the drippings fall for about five minutes. Coat the chicken lightly with honey. Leave it for ten minutes to let the honey dry on the chicken. Baste the chicken with ghee and put it back in the tandoor for ten minutes. When the skin is golden and crisp, garnish and serve.

Tandoori Chicken

*The mere mention of tandoori chicken induces
a passionate want. Then there is 'Tandoori Nights', a famous
BBC play! In London there seems to be a tandoori food joint
on every street, and numerous other tandoori restaurants
all over the world have not stopped mushrooming.*

Preparation and marination **7 ½ hours**
Cooking **25 minutes**

Broiler chicken	800 g

Marinade 1

Vinegar	2 tbsp
Red chilli powder	1/2 tbsp
Oil	3 tbsp
Salt	1 tsp

Marinade 2

Yoghurt	1 cup
Ginger paste	2 tbsp
Garlic paste	1 tbsp
Bay leaf	1
Cloves	2
Cardamom green	4
Mace	1/4 tsp
Nutmeg	1/4 tsp
Black peppercorns	1 tbsp
Caraway seeds	1 tsp
Red chillies	2
Oil	1 tbsp
Salt	1 tsp
Food colour	2 tsp

Basting

Ghee	1/4 cup

Garnish

Tandoori khatta masala
Onions
Green coriander chutney
Lemon

Clean the chicken. Make cuts on the breast and legs. Mix the ingredients of Marinade 1. Rub the mix all over the chicken. Leave aside for one hour.

Grind all the dry ingredients of Marinade 2. Then mix them with the rest of the ingredients, stir with a wooden spoon. Take a large bowl and pour in the marinade. Then place the chicken in it. Ideally the chicken should be well covered with the marinade. Roll it around by hand to effect permeation. Leave aside for six hours.

Oil and wipe the skewer. Skewer the chicken. Put the skewer into the tandoor and cook for ten minutes. Remove and stand upright against the tandoor to let the drippings fall for about five minutes. Baste the chicken and put it back into the tandoor for ten minutes. When ready, garnish and serve.

'Quick Fix' Tandoori Chicken

*This is the usual restaurant version that considers the need
for economy of time and for minimum loss of flavour.
The incredible part of the tandoor is that it functions as a
natural appliance for smoking. When the juices fall into the
bottom of a heated tandoor the smoking process commences—
an essential secret of tandoori flavour.*

Preparation and marination **3 ½ hours**
Cooking **20 minutes**

Broiler chicken whole*	800 g
Marinade	
Yoghurt	1/2 cup
Raw papaya paste	2 tbsp
Lemon juice	2 tbsp
Vinegar	1/4 cup
Ginger paste	2 tbsp
Garlic paste	1 tbsp
Garam masala	2 tsp
Red chilli powder	2 tsp
Cooking oil	1/4 cup
Salt	1 tsp
Food colour	1 tsp
Basting	
Cooking oil	1/2 cup
Garnish	
Tandoori khatta masala	
Lemon	
Green coriander chutney	
Pickled onion	

Clean the chicken. Make cuts on the breast and legs. Mix the ingredients of the marinade. Rub this mix all over the chicken. Leave aside for three hours.

Oil and wipe the skewer. Skewer the chicken. Put the skewer into the tandoor and cook for ten minutes. Remove and stand upright against the tandoor to let the drippings fall for about five minutes. Baste and put the skewer back into the tandoor for another five minutes. When ready, garnish and serve.

To cater to a steady stream of customers marination and first cooking for ten minutes can be done earlier and the skewers hung. When ordered they go into the tandoor and *voila* ! They are ready in five minutes.

* This recipe can be prepared with cut pieces of chicken as well.

Tandoori Game Birds

In my opinion it was the Indians who found natural ingredients to deodorize different kinds of meats. This deodorizing is very important to make some meats more palatable. For goose, duck or quail, it is almost obligatory. The best deodorizing ingredients include the flour of dried garbanzo split peas — called besan in India, and, of course, the ubiquitous garlic in the form of paste.

Preparation and marination **8 hours**
Cooking **25 minutes**

2 large birds or	800 g each	**Basting**	
4 small birds	400 g each	Oil	1 cup
Deodorizing 1		**Garnish**	
Garlic paste	2 tbsp	Mint yoghurt chutney	
Water	2¼ cup	Pickled onions	

Deodorizing 2
Chickpea flour — 2 cups

Marinade 1

Raw papaya paste	2 tbsp
Black pepper powder	1 tsp
Oil	3 tbsp
Salt	1 tsp

Marinade 2

Yoghurt	1 cup
Ginger paste	2 tbsp
Garlic paste	1 tbsp
Onion chopped	1½ cup
Caraway seed	1 tsp
Coriander seed	1/2 cup
Red chilli powder	1 tbsp
Nutmeg	1/2 tsp
Mace	1/2 tsp
Bay leaf	2
Cloves	4
Cardamom brown	4
Roasted Bengal gram flour	1/2 cup
Salt	2 tsp
Food colour	few drops

Clean the birds. Mix garlic paste and water and wash the birds thoroughly with this solution.

Divide the Deodorizing 2 ingredients into two parts. Rub the birds with one half and leave them aside for ten minutes. Then wash the birds in water and rub the birds again with the second half. After ten minutes, wash the birds again and pat them dry with a cloth.

Make cuts in the breast and legs. Mix the ingredients of Marinade 1. Coat the birds with the paste. Leave aside for one hour.

Fry the onions in the basting oil, till they are light brown. Drain and cool. Crush them by hand and keep aside. Roast the coriander. Then, along with all the other dry spices of Marinade 2, grind to a powder. Mix the garlic paste, ginger paste and yoghurt with the ground spices. To this add the roasted Bengal gram flour, crushed onions and food colour to form a uniformly thick marinade.

Black Partridge

Quail

Divide the marinade into two parts, one for each bird. Then divide each portion further into two. With one, coat the birds from the inside, and with the other, on the outside. Leave aside for five hours.

Oil and wipe the skewers. Skewer the birds, leaving a two inch gap between them. You can use an onion or a potato as a stopper between the birds. Put the skewers into the tandoor and cook for ten minutes. Remove and stand upright against the tandoor to let the drippings fall for about five minutes. Baste and put the skewers back into the tandoor for ten minutes. When ready, garnish and serve.

Red Jungle Fowl

Bar-headed Goose

Pin-tailed Duck

Tandoori Zeera Chicken

*For people like me who love zeera (cumin) this chicken
is always a favourite.*

Preparation and marination 6 ½ hours
Cooking 25 minutes

Broiler chicken cut in eight pieces	800 g
Marinade	
Yoghurt	1/2 cup
Ginger paste	1 tbsp
Garlic paste	2 tsp
Onion paste	1/2 cup
Cumin seed roasted and ground	1 tbsp
Coriander seeds roasted and ground	2 tsp
Red chilli powder	1 tsp
Oil	3 tbsp
Salt	1 tsp
Food colour	optional
Basting	
Ghee	1/4 cup
Garnish	
Zeerawala namak*	
Lemon	
Mixed vegetable pickle	

Clean the chicken pieces and make
cuts on the breast and legs. Mix all the
ingredients of the marinade and rub the
mix into the chicken pieces. Leave aside
for six hours, turning the pieces once
or twice in between.

Oil and wipe the skewers. Skewer
the chicken pieces. Put the skewers into
the tandoor and cook for ten minutes.
Remove and stand upright against the
tandoor to let the drippings fall for
about five minutes. Baste and put the
skewers back into the tandoor for five
to eight minutes. When ready, garnish
and serve.

*   Available at specialized outlets.

Dhania Coconut Chicken

Here is a bit of South India in the tandoori kitchen. I have experimented and found that the two kitchens complement each other well.

Preparation and marination **7 hours**
Cooking **25 minutes**

Broiler chicken tikka	1 kg

Marinade 1

Raw papaya paste	2 tbsp
Lemon juice	1/4 cup
Ginger paste	2 tbsp
Curry leaves chopped fine	2 tbsp
Green chilli paste	2 tbsp
Cooking oil	3 tbsp
Black pepper powder	2 tsp
Salt	tsp

Marinade 2

Yoghurt	1 cup
Coconut puree concentrated*	1/2 cup
Coriander seed roasted and ground**	3 tbsp

Basting

Oil	1/4 cup

Garnish

Green coriander chutney
Pickled onions

Wash, drain and dry the tikkas. Mix all the ingredients of Marinade 1 and put the tikkas in this. Leave aside for one hour.

Mix all the ingredients of Marinade 2 and put the tikkas in this and leave aside for five hours.

Oil and wipe the skewers. Skewer the tikkas. Put the skewers into the tandoor and cook for ten minutes. Remove and stand upright against the tandoor to let the drippings fall for about five minutes. Baste and put the skewers into the tandoor for ten minutes. When ready, garnish and serve.

*   Coconut puree can be fresh or readymade.

** Coriander should be ground with a little bit of yoghurt and not water.

Malai Chicken Tikka

The word 'malai' brings to mind a smooth and creamy texture, which is exactly what this dish has. The Oudh kitchen is famous for popularizing it.

Preparation and marination **7 ½ hours**
Cooking **25 minutes**

Broiler chicken tikka	1 kg

Marinade 1

Raw pineapple paste	1/4 cup
Green cardamom powdered	8
White pepper powdered	1 tbsp
Oil	1/4 cup
Salt	1 tsp

Marinade 2

Double cream	1/4 cup
Yoghurt	1 cup
Corn flour	1 tbsp
Amul cheese grated	2 tbsp
Peanut oil	3 tbsp
Ginger paste	2 tbsp
Garlic paste	1 tbsp
Green chillies minced	10
Green coriander minced	1/4 cup

Basting

Peanut oil	1/4 cup

Garnish

Onion rings
Green corinader chutney

Wash, drain and dry the tikkas. Mix all the ingredients of Marinade 1 and put the tikkas in this. Leave aside for half an hour.

Beat the cream and cheese together and mix with yoghurt and corn flour to make a smooth marinade. Add the rest of the ingredients of Marinade 2 to the above. Pour this over the tikkas. Mix well. Leave aside for six hours. For best results put into the freezer* for fifteen minutes before cooking.

Oil and wipe the skewers. Skewer the tikkas. Put the skewers into the tandoor and cook for ten minutes. Remove and stand upright against the tandoor to let the drippings fall for about five minutes. Baste and put the skewers back into the tandoor for ten minutes. When ready, garnish and serve.

* Keeping in the freezer hardens the creamy marinade so that it remains on the chicken when skewered.

Til Tikka

This flavour is quite exotic and would be wonderful for a sunny and lazy 'weekend lunch'.

Preparation and marination **6 hours**
Cooking **15 minutes**

Broiler chicken tikka	1 kg

Marinade 1

Yoghurt	1/2 cup
White vinegar	2 tbsp
Raw papaya paste	1 tbsp
Ellaichi jaiphal masala*	2 tsp
Black pepper ground	1 tsp
Oil	3 tbsp
Salt	1 tsp

Marinade 2

Eggs	3
Sesame seeds	1 cup
Green chillies minced	6
Green coriander minced	3/4 cup
Flour	1/2 cup
Salt	2 tsp
Food colour	optional

Basting

Oil	1/2 cup
Sesame oil	2 tsp

Garnish

Tomato chutney

Wash, drain and dry the tikkas. Mix all the ingredients of Marinade 1 and put the tikkas in this. Leave aside for five hours.

Beat the eggs, flour and salt in a flat dish and keep aside. Mix the sesame seeds, green chillies and coriander and spread these in another flat dish. Taking one tikka at a time, roll it in the egg mixture till well coated. Then roll in the sesame seed mix and put aside.

Oil and wipe the skewers. Skewer the tikkas as prepared, one at a time till all the skewers are ready. Put the skewers into the tandoor and cook for five minutes. Remove and stand upright against the tandoor to let the drippings fall for about five minutes. Mix the two basting oils. Baste and put the skewers back into the tandoor for five minutes. When ready, garnish and serve.

* See Basic Preparation.

Saffron Tikka

*Saffron — the aristocrat of spices — fragrant and
burnished gold in colour, straight from the Kashmir valley.*

Preparation and marination **6 ½ hours**
Cooking **20 minutes**

Broiler chicken tikka	1 kg
Marinade	
Raw papaya paste	2 tbsp
Yoghurt	1 cup
Saffron	1/4 tsp
Cardamom green powdered	8
Oil	3 tbsp
Salt	2 tsp
Basting	
Ghee	1/4 cup
Garnish	
Leftover marinade	
Almonds pounded	2 tbsp
Walnuts pounded	2 tbsp
Green coriander minced	1 tbsp

Wash, drain and dry the tikkas. Mix all ingredients of the marinade and put the tikkas into this. Turn the pieces well in the marinade so they are coated all around. Leave aside for six hours.

Oil and wipe the skewers. Skewer the tikkas. Put the skewers into the tandoor and cook for ten minutes. Remove and stand upright against the tandoor to let the drippings fall for about five minutes. Baste and put the skewers back into the tandoor for five minutes. When ready, garnish and serve.

To make the garnish chutney take the leftover marinade and mix it with the almonds, walnuts and green coriander. Heat on a slow fire till it is of a thickish consistency.

Saffron being weighed

Methi Tikka

Fresh green methi (fenugreek) blends wonderfully with chicken.
Unfortunately, in the North it is not available all year round
and we can enjoy it only for a few months of the year.

Preparation and marination **5 ½ hours**
Cooking **20 minutes**

Broiler chicken tikka	1 kg
Marinade 1	
White vinegar	1/4 cup
Ginger paste	2 tbsp
Garlic paste	1 tbsp
White pepper ground	1 tsp
Oil	3 tbsp
Marinade 2	
Hung yoghurt	1/2 cup
Coriander powder	1 tbsp
Fenugreek green leaves(minced)	2 tbsp
Corn flour	3 tbsp
Chickpea flour	1 tbsp
Salt	2 tsp
Food colour	optional
Basting	
Ghee	1/4 cup
Fenugreek seeds	1/2 tsp
Small ball of wheat flour dough	walnut size
Garnish	
Onion rings	
Lemon	
Garam masala	

Wash, drain and dry the tikkas. Mix all the ingredients of Marinade 1 and put the tikkas into this. Leave aside for four hours.

Mix all the ingredients of Marinade 2 and put the marinated tikkas into this. Leave aside for one hour.

Heat the basting ghee in a small frying pan. Take the ball of wheat flour dough (atta) and stick the fenugreek seeds onto it. When the ghee is hot put this ball in, and let it sizzle till the seeds are brown. Remove this ball from the ghee. You now have basting ghee with a gentle fragrance of fenugreek.

Oil and wipe the skewers. Skewer five or six pieces of tikkas closely together. Then place a piece of potato (quartered from a large potato), again skewer five or six pieces of chicken and put a piece of potato and so on. Generally two sets of tikkas will fit on one skewer. Put the skewers into the tandoor and cook for ten minutes. Remove and stand upright against the tandoor to let the drippings fall, for about five minutes. Baste with the prepared ghee and put the skewers back into the tandoor for five minutes. When ready, garnish and serve.

Shoofta Thandai

*Whenever we made thandai on Holi, I always wondered
if the typical masalas would blend with other types of food.
Here is an innovation — minus the bhang !*

Preparation and marination	**4 ½ hours**
Cooking	**20 minutes**

Broiler chicken mince	500 g

Marinade 1

Raw papaya paste	1 tbsp
Red chilli powder	1 tsp
Cooking oil	2 tbsp

Marinade 2

Thandai mix ground*	3 tbsp
Ginger paste	1 tsp
Green chillies minced	2
Green coriander minced	1 tbsp
Fresh rose petals crushed	a few
Corn flour	2 tbsp
Roasted Bengal gram flour	1/2 cup
Salt	1 tsp

Basting

Ghee or oil	1/4 cup

Garnish

Green coriander chutney

Mix all the ingredients of Marinade 1 and add them to the mince. Leave aside for three hours.

Mix the ingredients of Marinade 2, and add these to the marinated mince. Leave aside for one hour.

Oil and wipe the skewers. Press mince into sausage-shaped kababs directly onto the skewers. Put the skewers into the tandoor and cook for eight minutes. Remove and stand upright against tandoor to let the drippings fall for about five minutes. Baste and put the skewers back in the tandoor for five minutes. When ready, garnish and serve.

* Readymade thandai mix is available. If it is to be prepared fresh, see glossary of names.

Poppy Flower

Recipe photograph overleaf

Badami Kabab

*Badam (almonds) give a soft texture and a special
fragrance to food, adding a subtle touch of luxury. This recipe
evokes just that mood.*

Preparation and marination 5 ½ hours
Cooking 20 minutes

Broiler chicken mince	500 g
Marinade 1	
Raw pineapple paste	2 tbsp
Red chilli powder	1 tbsp
Oil	1 tbsp
Marinade 2	
Almonds skinned and pasted*	3/4 cup
Cardamom green powdered	3
Garam masala	2 tsp
Cornflour	1/4 cup
Salt	1 tsp
Basting	
Oil	1/4 cup
Garnish	
Yoghurt	1/4 cup
Onions pounded	1 tbsp
Almonds pounded	1 tbsp
Green chillies chopped fine	2
Green mint leaves	
chopped fine	1 tsp
Zeerawala namak	1 tsp

Mix all the ingredients of Marinade 1 and add them to the mince. Leave aside for one hour.

Mix the ingredients of Marinade 2 and add these to the marinated mince. Leave aside for four hours.

Oil and wipe the skewers. Press mince into sausage-shaped kababs directly onto the skewers. Put the skewers into the tandoor and cook for eight minutes. Remove and stand upright against the tandoor to let the drippings fall for about five minutes. Baste and put the skewers back into the tandoor for five minutes. When ready, garnish and serve.

To prepare garnish mix all the ingredients into the yoghurt.

*   No water should be used
when making this paste of almonds.
The traditional Indian silbatta is ideal.

Mewa Kabab

Two 'annas' a handful or pocketful, whichever was bigger
— mewa or dry fruit was a childhood joy. Recreating the mood
here is a rich kabab for special occassions !

Preparation and marination **6 hours**
Cooking **20 minutes**

Broiler chicken mince	500 g

Marinade

Kachri powder*	1 tbsp
Ginger paste	1 tbsp
Garlic paste	2 tsp
Green chillies minced	2 tsp
Green coriander minced	1 tbsp
Pistachio whole	1 tsp
Cashewnut whole	1 tbsp
Almonds skinned	6 to 8
Sultanas minced	10
Chironji	2 tbsp
Watermelon seeds	1 tbsp
Nutmeg powder	a pinch
Mace powder	a pinch
Bread crumbs	1/2 cup
Oil	2 tbsp
Salt	1 tsp

Basting

Oil	1/4 cup

Garnish

Lemon juice
Peanut cabbage relish

Roast watermelon seeds and chironji separately. Cool. Mix these with all the ingredients of the marinade apart from the bread crumbs, oil and salt. Grind to a granular consistency. Add the bread crumbs oil and salt and mix with the chicken mince. Leave aside for five hours.

Oil and wipe the skewers. Press mince into sausage-shaped kababs directly onto the skewers. Put the skewers into the tandoor and cook for ten minutes. Remove and stand upright against the tandoor to let the drippings fall for about five minutes. Baste and put the skewers back in the tandoor for five minutes. When ready, garnish and serve.

* See glossary of names.

Cocktail Kabab

*A great recipe for a snack! One must calculate the
quantity well, as people will usually eat more than you expect.*

Preparation and marination **4 ½ hours**
Cooking **20 minutes**

Broiler chicken mince	500 g

Marinade 1

Raw papaya paste	1 tbsp
Raw mango powder	2 tsp
White pepper ground	1 tbsp
Oil	2 tbsp

Marinade 2

Onion fried and pasted	1/4 cup
Red chillies coarse ground	1 tsp
Green coriander minced	1 tbsp
White sesame seeds	3 tbsp
Cornflakes ground	1/4 cup
Salt	1 tsp

Basting

Ghee or cooking oil	1/4 cup

Garnish

Til chutney
Mixed green relish

Mix all the ingredients of Marinade 1 with the chicken mince. Leave this aside for three hours.

Mix all the ingredients of Marinade 2 and add these to the marinated mince. Knead well and leave aside for an hour.

Oil and wipe the skewers. Press mince into sausage-shaped kababs directly onto the skewers. Put the skewers into the tandoor and cook for ten minutes. Remove and stand upright against tandoor to let the drippings fall for about five minutes. Baste and put the skewers into the tandoor for five minutes. When ready, garnish and serve.

Lamb

 Sheep and goats were amongst the earliest animals to be domesticated by man nearly 11,000 years ago. Today, the succulence and flavour of lamb make it the more popular meat. The age of the lamb can be anywhere between six months to two years. A reliable butcher is the best advisor and guide when preparing any particular lamb recipe.

Lamb kababs, in particular, are delicious. The word 'kab' implies a turning movement in Arabic. In Persian, 'Cabob' means roasted or grilled, and 'kam aab', with little water or semi-dry. Any or all of these combined could have given rise to the word 'kabab'. Certainly, kababs are almost universal and every nation lays claims to their origin.

There were two famous kababias I can recall during my early days in Delhi. Masita was one, based in Meerut (U.P.) before he shifted to Delhi and set up his kabab shop at Jama Masjid. Tunda, who made and sold his kababs in Lucknow, was the other. Unfortunately, as so often happens, both these great kabab experts never shared their recipes and so their secrets died with them. I have tried to recreate some of the old recipes, but I doubt that they can ever match the great Masita kababs or Tunda kababs.

Tender, lean meat from the hindquater, usually referred to as 'prime cut' is the best for kababs. In addition, apart from the two basic cuts, tikka and mince, that are common to poultry, lamb and fish, lamb has a number of other cuts that play a critical role when cooking tandoori food.

Ran	Upper part of the hind leg.
Chops	A chop is a one to one-and a-half inch thick piece of meat with a bone. The chop is beaten to help tenderizing. The type included here are rib chops. The recipe indicates whether they are three-rib or two-rib chops.
Shoulder	The upper portion of the shoulder with fat. This may be sold boned or with bone and is excellent for roasting.
Pasanday	These are pieces, four to five inch long and one inch thick from the fore or hind leg of lamb. They are beaten to half their thickness and scored on one side in a criss-cross pattern to facilitate tenderizing.
Strips	Flank steak cut diagonally across the grain and beaten to make four to five inch strips.
Tikka	Approximately two inch cubes or irregular pieces from the fore or hind leg of lamb. This meat is without fat.
Marbled	Upper part of shoulder or breast meat with fat.
Mince	Meat from the hind leg of lamb free from fat and gristle, generally run through the mincer or hand chopped.

Before marination the meat should always be washed and drained well. After which it should be dried with a kitchen towel and put into the marinade. Meat to be made into mince should be washed before being ground. Once it is ground it should not be put into water.

Tikka, marbled meat and mince

Ran and chop

Shoulder, pasanday and strips

Ran-Nawabi

Whole leg of lamb, tenderized and precooked, is a great time saver; it is so soft you can scoop it up with a spoon.

Preparation and marination **5 ½ hours**
Cooking **25 minutes**

Leg of lamb	1–1 ½ kg
Potato	1

For Boiling

Onion large	1
Garlic cloves	4
Ginger	1" piece
Black peppercorns	1 tbsp
Salt	2 tsp

Marinade

Hung yoghurt	3 tbsp
Lemon juice	2 tbsp
Ginger grated	1 tsp
Green coriander minced	2 tbsp
Coriander roasted and ground	2 tbsp
Cumin roasted and ground	1 tsp
Red chilli powder	1 tbsp
Nutmeg powder	1/2 tsp
Oil	1/2 cup
Salt	2 tsp

Basting

Ghee	1/4 cup
Saffron	1/4 tsp
Silver foil*	a few

Garnish

Green mint chutney
Pickled onions

Chop the onion and ginger coarsely. Wash the leg and boil it with other ingredients for half an hour. Let the leg cool. Take it out of the pan and make deep cuts in it to enable the marinade to penetrate. Mix all the ingredients of the marinade and rub well into the leg. Leave aside for four-and a-half hours.

Oil and wipe the skewer and skewer the leg. Tie the bone of the leg to the skewer and skewer the potato after the leg. This will hold the leg in place. Put the skewer into the tandoor and cook for ten minutes. Remove the skewers. Baste the leg and put the skewers back into the tandoor for ten minutes. When ready, put the silver foil on the leg. Garnish and serve.

* See glossary of names.

Ran Mussalam

Kachri and raw papaya are two well-known tenderizers. When cooking a whole leg in the tandoor tenderizing is very important, hence the use of three tenderizers. The tender leg of a lamb will make this dish unbelievably soft.

Preparation and marination **12 hours**
Cooking **40 minutes**

Leg of Lamb	1kg

Marinade

Hung yoghurt	1/2 cup
Raw papaya paste	2 tbsp
Kachri ground*	2 tsp
Vinegar	1/2 cup
Ginger paste	3 tbsp
Garlic paste	2 tbsp
Fried onion paste	1/4 cup
Garam masala	1 tbsp
Red chilli powder	1 tbsp
Figs pounded	4
Almond paste	2 tbsp
Oil	1/2 cup
Salt	2 tsp

Basting

Ghee	1/2 cup

Garnish

Tandoori khatta masala
Lemon
Onion rings

Make deep cuts in the leg of lamb to enable the marinade to penetrate. Mix all the ingredients of the marinade apart from the salt and rub well into the leg. Leave aside for eleven hours. Add the salt and turn the leg well. Keep for fifteen minutes.

Suspend the leg on a hook and chain arrangement or skewer right through with two skewers. Put into the tandoor and cook for ten minutes. Remove the skewers and leave suspended to let the drippings fall for about five minutes. Baste the leg and put back into the tandoor for ten minutes. Repeat the process once more. When ready garnish and serve.

Check during the second cooking to see if the leg is done to satisfaction.

* See glossary of names.

Scoring the shoulder

Marination

Shoulder with stuffing and support stick

Rolled shoulder

Rolled and tied shoulder

Cooked shoulder

Sliced shoulder kababs

Shoulder Kabab

*Roast shoulder is associated with very few ingredients. Filled
with masala and put in the tandoor, it makes a delicious dish.*

Preparation and marination **7 hours**
Cooking **25 Minutes**

Shoulder of lamb	500–700 g
Potato	1

Marinade

Raw papaya paste	1 tbsp
Vinegar	1/4 cup
Yoghurt	1/2 cup
White pepper ground	1 tbsp
Ginger paste	1 tbsp
Garlic paste	2 tsp
Oil	1/4 cup
Salt	1 tsp

Stuffing

Green chillies minced	4
Large onion minced	1
Indian cottage cheese loose	1 cup
Elaichi jaiphal masala	1/2 tsp
Corn flour	1/4 cup
Egg	1
Salt	1 tsp

Basting

Oil	1/4 cup
Left over marinade	1

Garnish

Til chutney
Elaichi jaiphal masala
Lemon

Wash, drain and dry the shoulder meat,
flatten with a wooden mallet. Score it
from the inside. Mix all the ingredients
of the marinade apart from the salt and
rub into the shoulder on both sides.
Leave aside for six hours. Add the salt
and keep for another fifteen minutes.

Rub the cottage cheese and corn
flour together. Then mix all the other
ingredients of the stuffing. It should
become a uniform mix. Remove the
shoulder from the marinade and spread
it out flat. At one end place a long
sausage-shaped roll of the stuffing. Take
a thin twig of neem* and place it along
the roll. Start rolling the shoulder from
this end. Tie up the roll securely.

Oil and wipe the skewer. Skewer
the shoulder along the twig and skewer
the potato after it. Put the skewer into
the tandoor and cook for ten minutes.
Remove and stand upright against the
tandoor to let the drippings fall for
about five minutes. Baste the shoulder
and put the skewer back in the tandoor
for ten minutes. When ready, take the
shoulder roll off the skewer. Remove
the twig and cut into one-inch thick
slices. Garnish and serve.

*   Use a twig from any herbal plant
    if neem is not available.

*Photographs of step by step technique on
previous pages*

Dhania Adrak Chop

For those who like ginger, this chop will be irresistible.
The green of the spinach adds an authentic touch.

Preparation and marination **9 hours**
Cooking **25 minutes**

Two rib lamb chops, one bone
  removed   1 kg

Marinade

Yoghurt	1 cup
Raw papaya paste	3 tbsp
Ginger paste	1 tbsp
Green coriander paste	1 tbsp
Green chilli paste	1 tbsp
Fresh spinach puree	1/4 cup
Ginger grated fine	2 tbsp
Oil	1/4 cup
Salt	2 tsp

Basting

Oil	1/2 cup

Garnish

Yoghurt salad
Pickled onions

Wash and drain the chops. Pat them dry. Beat them with a wooden mallet. Mix all the ingredients of the marinade other than the salt. Put the chops into this marinade. Leave aside for eight hours. Add the salt and keep for another fifteen minutes.

Oil and wipe the skewers. Skewer the chops and put the skewers into the tandoor and cook for ten minutes. Remove and stand upright against the tandoor to let the drippings fall for about five minutes. Baste the chops and put the skewers back into the tandoor for another ten minutes. Check once in between. When ready, garnish and serve.

Masala Chops

Curry has always been a great favourite in the West.
Chops marinated in curry masala and cooked in the tandoor
add a new dimension to the flavour.

Preparation and marination **9 hours**
Cooking **20 minutes**

Lamb chops two ribbed, one bone removed	1 kg

Marinade

Yoghurt	1 cup
Vinegar	2 tbsp
Ginger paste	2 tbsp
Garlic paste	1 tbsp
Green chilli paste	2 tsp
Green coriander minced	3 tbsp
Curry masala	4 tsp
Carum seed	1 tsp
Turmeric powder	1 tsp
Oil	1/4 cup
Salt	2 tsp

Basting

Ghee or oil	1/2 cup

Garnish

Tomato chutney

Wash and drain the chops. Pat them dry. Beat them with a wooden mallet.

Heat the oil in a shallow pan. Mix all the ingredients of marinade other than salt and add this to the oil, stir for a few minutes. Now cool the mixture. Leave the chops in this marinade for eight hours, turning over twice or thrice in between. Add the salt and keep for another fifteen minutes.

Oil and wipe the skewers. Skewer the chops. Put the skewers into the tandoor and cook for ten minutes. Remove and stand upright against the tandoor to let the drippings fall for about five minutes. Baste the chops and put the skewers back into the tandoor for five minutes. When ready, garnish and serve.

Kabargah

This is an adaptation of a very popular Kashmiri recipe.
The kind you would like to take with you 'beyond the grave'.

Preparation and marination **3 hours**
Cooking **15 minutes**

Three rib lamb chops	
2 bones removed	1 kg

For Boiling

Milk	2 cups
Water	1 cup
Bay leaf	1
Aniseed	1 tsp
Black peppercorns	1 tbsp
Red chilli powder	1 tsp
Cardamom green	4
Cloves	2

Marinade 1

Salt	2 tsp

Marinade 2 (Batter)

Eggs	2
Yoghurt	1 cup
Red chilli powder	2 tsp
Corn flour	1/4 cup
Salt	1 tsp

Basting

Ghee	1/2 cup
Saffron	1/4 tsp
Milk	1 tbsp

Garnish

Green mint chutney

Set the water to boil and add the ingredients. Wash and drain the chops. Put them in the boiling water till they are tender and the liquid has dried up. Remove from the pan, and sprinkle salt (Marinade 1) over them. Leave aside for twenty minutes.

Make a batter with the ingredients of Marinade 2 and coat the chops well. Leave aside for one hour.

Oil and wipe the skewers. Skewer the chops and put the skewers into the tandoor and cook for five minutes. Remove and baste the kababs with melted ghee followed by basting with saffron soaked in milk. Put the chops back into the tandoor for five minutes. When ready, garnish and serve.

Pasanda Panir

A highly specialised meat cut, not always available. For good results, patronize a shop that sells the best quality pasandas.

Preparation and marination **7 hours**
Cooking **20 minutes**

Pasanda pieces 4"x 5"	1 kg
Indian cottage cheese	
pieces 2"x 1"x 1/2"	15 to 20
Green chillies	15 to 20
Green coriander chutney	1/4 cup

Marinade

Yoghurt	1 cup
Raw papaya paste	2 tbsp
Ginger paste	2 tbsp
Garlic paste	1 tbsp
Almond paste	2 tbsp
Green coriander chopped	2 tbsp
Coriander seeds roasted	
and ground	2 tbsp
Cardamoms green ground	4
Red chilli powder	2 tsp
Saffron	a pinch
Oil	1/4 cup
Salt	2 tsp
Food colour	optional

Basting

Ghee or oil	1/2 cup

Garnish

Green coriander chutney
White radish relish

Mix all the ingredients of the marinade other than salt and put the pasandas in this. Leave aside for six hours. Mix the cottage cheese pieces with the marinated pasandas and add the salt. Leave aside for fifteen minutes.

Oil and wipe the skewers. Skewer one pasanda, one or two strips of paneer, one green chilli and brush with a little green coriander chutney. Then add another pasanda, cottage cheese, etc., till you have about two sets like this packed tightly together on one skewer. Now frame each group of five with thin bamboo sticks and tie with some kitchen string.

Baste and put the skewers into the tandoor and cook for ten minutes. Remove and stand upright against tandoor to let the drippings fall for about five minutes. Baste and put the skewers back into the tandoor for five minutes. When ready, garnish and serve.

Laberian

Pronounced Le-be-rian, this is an Urdu term used for a very interesting cut of lamb meat. The strips, skewered and cooked, make a good variation.

Preparation and marination **5 hours**
Cooking **25 minutes**

Lamb pieces 5"x 2"x 1"	1 kg

Marinade 1

Lemon juice	1/2 cup
Raw pineapple paste	3 tbsp
Garlic paste	1 tbsp
Black pepper powder	2 tsp
Oil	1/4 cup

Marinade 2

Yoghurt	1 cup
Green chillies minced	6 to 8
Peanuts roasted and ground	3/4 cup
Green coriander minced	1 tbsp
Salt	2 tsp

Basting

Oil	1/2 cup

Garnish

Tandoori khatta masala
Onion rings
Lemon

Mix all the ingredients of Marinade 1. Put the strips into this and mix. Leave aside for one hour.

Make a uniform mix of the ingredients of Marinade 2 other than the salt. Put the strips in this and leave aside for three hours. Add the salt and leave aside for another fifteen minutes.

Oil and wipe the skewers. Skewer the strips, threading through very much like running a needle through a piece of cloth. Put the skewers into the tandoor and cook for ten minutes. Remove and stand upright against tandoor to let the drippings fall for about five minutes. Baste the strips and put the skewers back into the tandoor for five minutes. When ready, garnish and serve.

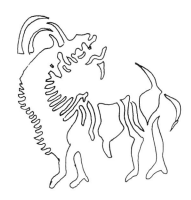

Kufli Kabab

*My great-grandfather Sir Ganga Ram's house in Lahore was
a meeting place for many interesting personalities. One elderly
lady who shared a common interest in food with my father was
gracious enough to give him this recipe she had inherited from
her ancestral house of Oudh. Kufal in Urdu means to lock in.
Here we are actually locking in the flavour of the meat with batter.*

Preparation and marination **7 hours**
Cooking **20 minutes**

Strips cut lengthwise	1 kg
Oil	1/4 cup
Marinade	
Raw papaya paste	1/4 cup
Ginger paste	2 tbsp
Fried onion paste	1/2 cup
Green chilli paste	2 tsp
Walnut minced	2 tsp
Apricot dried and minced	2 tsp
Pine nuts minced	2 tsp
Garam masala	2 tsp
Caraway seed roasted	1 tsp
Red chilli powder	2 tsp
Oil	1/4 cup
Salt	2 tsp
Batter	
Yoghurt	1 cup
Green chillies minced	5
Almond paste	1/4 cup
Garam masala	1/2 tsp
Flour	1/2 cup
Egg	1
Salt	1 tsp
Basting	
Oil	1/4 cup

Garnish
Til chutney
Pickled vegetables
Lemon juice

Mix all the ingredients of the marinade other than the salt, and put the strips into this. Leave aside for six hours. Heat the oil in a pan and add the marinated meat strips and salt. Fry on high heat for five minutes. Take out from oil and cool.

Whisk all ingredients for the batter together to a uniform smoothness.

Oil and wipe the skewers. Skewer the strips and push the ends of the strips together. In other words gather each strip together. Skewer all the strips. Coat them with batter mix. When all the skewers are ready put them into the tandoor and cook for five minutes. Remove, baste the kababs. Put the skewers back into the tandoor again. When the coating of batter starts turning golden brown remove, garnish and serve.

Bhaditraka

*Manasollasa was written by Somesvara in AD 1127 for
the royal kitchens. It is one of the few 'cookbooks' to have
survived nearly 900 years. One particular recipe for meat says:*

*'When pieces of clean meat, bored with some holes
and filled with spices, were roasted on spits, and some more
spices were added, they were called Bhaditraka'.*

Manas. III. 1462-68

Given below is my translation of this recipe.

Preparation and marination 8 ½ hours
Cooking 25 minutes

Boneless tikka	500 g
Marinade	
Lemon juice	2 tbsp
Raw papaya paste	2 tbsp
Ginger paste	1 tbsp
Onion paste	1/4 cup
Green chilli paste	1 tsp
Black pepper ground	2 tsp
Nutmeg powder	1/2 tsp
Cardamom green powdered	1 tsp
Turmeric powder	1/2 tsp
Oil	3 tbsp
Salt	1 tsp
Basting	
Leftover marinade	
Ghee or oil	1/2 cup
Garnish	
Elaichi jaiphal masala	
Lemon	
Mixed vegetable pickle	

Mix all the ingredients of the marinade other than the salt, and put the tikkas in it. Leave aside for eight hours. Add the salt and leave aside for another fifteen minutes.

Oil and wipe the skewers. Skewer the tikkas. Baste with leftover marinade. Put the skewers into the tandoor and cook for ten minutes. Remove and stand upright against tandoor to let the drippings fall for about five minutes. Baste the tikkas again and put the skewers back into the tandoor for five to eight minutes. When ready, garnish and serve.

Kandupacita Mamsa

*There are abundant ancient records that lead me
to believe that Hindus in those times had their typical
meat recipes for the kandu or tandoor.*

Preparation and marination **8 ½ hours**
Cooking **25 minutes**

Boneless tikka	500 g

Marinade

Yoghurt	1 cup
Raw papaya paste	2 tbsp
Vinegar	1/4 cup
Ginger paste	1 tbsp
Garlic paste	1 tsp
Onion paste	1/4 cup
Saurabh (coriander powder)	2 tbsp
Rajika (mustard powder)	1 tbsp
Red chilli powder	2 tsp
Oil	1/4 cup
Salt	1 tsp

Basting

Ghee	1/4 cup

Garnish

Mint yoghurt chutney

Mix all the ingredients of the marinade other than the salt, and put the tikkas in it. Leave aside for eight hours. The meat can be turned a couple of times for better marination. Add the salt and leave aside for another fifteen minutes.

Oil and wipe the skewers. Skewer the tikkas. Put the skewers into the tandoor and cook for ten minutes. Remove and stand upright against tandoor to let the drippings fall for about five minutes. Baste the tikkas and put the skewers back into the tandoor for another ten minutes. When ready garnish and serve.

Recipe photograph on previous page

Tikka Mughlai

In every land, there is a king who is special.
This is my 'special', fit for a king — the Mughlai Tikka.

Preparation and marination **8 ½ hours**
Cooking **25 minutes**

Boneless tikka made from marbled meat	500 g
Marinade	
Yoghurt	1 cup
Raw papaya paste	2 tbsp
Ginger paste	2 tbsp
Garlic paste	1 tbsp
Almond paste	2 tbsp
Pistachio paste	2 tbsp
Aromatic garam masala	1/2 tbsp
Caraway seed	1 tsp
Red chilli powder	1 tsp
Corn flour	3 tbsp
Oil	3 tbsp
Salt	1 tsp
Basting	
Oil	1/4 cup
Garnish	
Leftover marinade	
Saffron	a pinch
Milk	1 tbsp
Mint leaves chopped	1/2 tsp

Mix all the ingredients of the marinade other than the salt, and put the tikkas in it. Leave aside for eight hours. Add the salt and leave aside for another fifteen minutes.

Oil and wipe the skewers. Skewer the tikkas and baste them. Put the skewers into the tandoor and cook for ten minutes. Remove and stand upright against tandoor to let drippings fall for about five minutes. Baste the tikkas again and put the skewers back into the tandoor for five to eight minutes. When ready, garnish and serve.

To prepare the garnish soak the saffron in milk. On a slow flame heat the leftover marinade. When it begins to thicken, add the saffron soaked in milk and cook for a couple of minutes. Sprinkle with mint leaves and serve.

Recipe photograph overleaf

163

Tikka Kandahari

The areas of Kabul and Kandahar are well known for their meat recipes. Here is 'Tikka Kandahari', the 'Kuku masi' favourite. Traditional gora, dried sour grape powder, has been substituted with amchur for garnishing.

Preparation and marination **8 ½ hours**
Cooking **25 minutes**

Boneless tikka made from marbled meat	500 g

Marinade

Raw papaya diced	1/2 cup
Kachri ground*	2 tsp
Yoghurt	1/2 cup
Double cream	1/2 cup
Ginger paste	1 tbsp
Garlic paste	2 tsp
Black pepper powder	1 tbsp
Cardamom green ground	1/2 tsp
Garam masala	2 tsp
Red chilli powder	1 tsp
Oil	3 tbsp
Salt	1 tsp

Basting

Oil	1/4 cup

Garnish

Raw mango powder/gora
Onion rings
Lemon

Mix all the ingredients of the marinade other than the salt, and put the tikkas in it. Leave aside for eight hours. Add the salt and leave aside for another fifteen minutes.

Oil and wipe the skewers. Skewer the tikkas and baste. Put the skewers into the tandoor and cook for ten minutes. Remove and stand upright against tandoor to let the drippings fall for about five minutes. Baste the tikkas again and put the skewers back into the tandoor for five to eight minutes. When ready, garnish and serve.

*   See glossary of names.

Boti Din Raat

*This delicious innovative recipe very naturally moves
to centre stage as a conversation piece!*

Preparation and marination **8 ½ hours**
Cooking **20 minutes**

Boneless tikka	500 g
Marinade	
Raw papaya paste	3 tbsp
Yoghurt	1 cup
Ginger paste	2 tsp
Garlic paste	1 tsp
Onion paste	1/4 cup
Black pepper powder	1 tsp
Cardamom green ground	1 tsp
Saffron	1/2 tsp
Milk	1 tsp
Oil	1/4 cup
Salt	1 tsp
Finishing	
Hard-boiled eggs	10
Basting	
Oil	1/4 cup
Garnish	
Mustard chutney	
Mixed green relish	

Soak the saffron in milk for a few minutes. Mix all the ingredients of the marinade other than the salt and put the tikkas in it. Leave aside for eight hours. Add the salt and leave aside for another fifteen minutes.

Peel and cut the hard-boiled eggs in half. Remove the yolks and set aside.

Oil and wipe the skewers. Skewer the tikkas and put the skewers into the tandoor and cook for ten minutes. Remove and stand upright against the tandoor to let the drippings fall for about five minutes. Baste the tikkas and put the skewers back in the tandoor for five minutes. When ready remove from the skewers and fill into the hollowed egg. Serve hot with other garnishes.

*An interesting side dish can be made with the egg yolks
to be served along with the garnish. For this you need:*

Egg yolk	10
Onion minced fine	2
Green chillies chopped fine	4
Oil	2 tsp
Green coriander chopped fine	2 tbsp
Salt	to taste
Black pepper	to taste
Lemon juice	2 tbsp

Chop the egg yolk coarsely and mix lightly with other ingredients, sprinkle with salt and pepper. Squeeze the lemon and serve.

Hing Kabab

*Pre-cooked meat kababs are delicious and great
time savers. Do try this recipe.*

Preparation and marination · **3 hours**
Cooking **15 minutes**

Boneless tikka	1 kg

For boiling

Turmeric powder	1 tsp
Black peppercorns	1 tsp
Mace powder	1 tsp
Nutmeg powder	1/2 tsp
Bay leaf	2
Cloves	2
Oil	3 tbsp
Water	4 cups
Salt	2 tsp

Marinade 1

Oil	1/2 cup
Asafoetida (compounded powder)	1 tsp

Marinade 2

Cumin roasted and ground	2 tsp
Coriander roasted and ground	2 tsp
Ginger dry powder	1 tsp
Raw mango powder	1tsp
Yoghurt	1 cup

Basting

Ghee	1/4 cup

Garnish

Tomato chutney
Pickled onions

Wash the tikkas and put them in boiling water along with all the masalas. Boil for fifteen minutes. Drain the pieces and fry lightly with Marinade 1 masala. Once they are light brown, they can be kept aside and cooled.

Mix all ingredients of Marinade 2. Soak the tikkas in this for two hours or till required for serving.

Oil and wipe the skewers. Skewer the tikkas and put the skewers into the tandoor and cook for ten minutes. Remove the skewers and check if further cooking is required. If so, baste the tikkas and put the skewers back into the tandoor for five minutes. When ready, garnish and serve.

Sidhi Sadhi Seekh

The seekh kabab is one of the most well-known tandoori dishes. There are a number of a recipes for seekh today, each cook adding his own ingredients to give a special taste. This is one of the most basic recipes. As you go along you will find more variations in this book.

Preparation and marination **6 hours**
Cooking **20 minutes**

Mince	500 g
Marinade	
Raw papaya paste	2 tbsp
Ginger paste	2 tbsp
Fried onion paste	1/2 cup
Green chillies minced	3
Garam masala	1 tsp
Red chilli powder	1 tsp
Split chickpea flour	1 cup
Egg	1
Oil	2 tbsp
Salt	1 tsp
Turmeric powder	optional
Basting	
Ghee or oil	1/4 cup
Garnish	
Tandoori khatta masala	
Onion rings	

Grind the mince once. Drain any excess juice of the raw papaya paste and ginger. Deep fry the onion and make a paste. Mix these with the chillies, garam masala and oil and add to the mince. The mixture should be as dry* as possible. Leave aside for five hours. Half an hour before cooking add the split chickpea flour, egg and salt. Mix the ingredients well.

Oil and wipe the skewers, press mince into sausage-shaped kababs directly into the skewers. Put the skewers into the tandoor and cook for ten minutes. Remove and stand upright against tandoor to let the drippings fall for about five minutes. Baste the kababs and put them back into the tandoor for another five minutes. When ready, garnish and serve.

*   Dry means lacking any water content.

171

Bukni Kabab

As the name suggests, this is a hot and spicy kabab.
Bukni is pounded red chilli; the traditional chilli powder.
While pounding, a few drops of mustard oil are added to make
the process easier. The mustard acts as a preservative in
addition to enhancing the red colour of chilli.

Preparation and marination **7 hours**
Cooking **20 minutes**

Mince	500g

Marinade 1

Papaya paste	2 tbsp
Ginger paste	1 tsp
Bukni	2 tbsp
Oil	2 tbsp
Food colour	optional

Marinade 2

Chironji roasted	1 tbsp
Ginger grated	1 tbsp
Onion minced and drained	1/4 cup
Green coriander minced	2 tbsp
Roasted Bengal gram flour	1/4 cup
Egg	1
Salt	2 tsp

Basting

Ghee or oil	1/4 cup

Garnish

Peanut chutney
Onion rings
Lemon

Grind the mince twice. Mix all the ingredients of Marinade 1 with the mince. Leave aside for five hours.

Put aside the gram-flour, egg and salt. Grind all the other ingredients of Marinade 2. Mix these with the mince and again leave aside for one hour to enable the flavours to be absorbed. Beat the egg, add the gram-flour and salt. Blend this mixture with the marinated mince.

Oil and wipe the skewers. Press mince into sausage-shaped kababs directly onto the skewers. Put the skewers into the tandoor and cook for eight minutes. Remove and stand upright against tandoor to let the drippings fall for about five minutes. Baste the kababs and put the skewers back into the tandoor for another five minutes. When ready, garnish and serve.

Kakori Kabab

Situated on the banks of the Gomti, steeped in the traditions of Oudh, Kakori is a place well known for its revolutionaries and for its kababs. It is here that the famous kakori kababs originated.

Preparation and marination   **4 ½ hours**
Cooking **30 minutes**

Mince from marbled meat	1 kg
Marinade	
Cardamom green seed	1 tsp
Cardamom brown seed	1 tsp
Black pepper ground	2 tbsp
Cloves	1/2 tsp
Nutmeg pounded	1 tsp
Roasted Bengal gramflour	2 cup
Fried onion paste	1/2 cup
Green chillies minced	5
Eggs	2
Oil	1/4 cup
Salt	2 tsp
Basting	
Ghee	1/2 cup
Garnish	
Ghee melted*	1/4 cup
Keora	few drops
Green coriander chutney	
Onion rings	
Lemon	

Grind the mince twice. Grind and mix the ingredients of the marinade other than the gramflour, eggs and salt. Rub well into the mince. The process of rubbing in is important as all the ingredients have to blend well with the mince. Leave aside for four hours. Add the gram-flour, eggs and salt and leave aside for fifteen minutes.

Oil and wipe the skewers. Press mince into sausage-shaped kababs directly onto the skewers, and baste the kabas. Put the skewers into the tandoor and cook for eight minutes. Remove and stand upright against tandoor to let the drippings fall for about five minutes. Baste the kababs again and put the skewers back into the tandoor for five minutes. When ready, pour melted hot ghee and a few drops of keora essence onto the kababs. Serve with other garnishes.

*   This ghee is leftover from basting.

Recipe photograph overleaf

Kabab Do Rukha Seekh Par

The unique flavour of this kabab is derived from a combination of two distinct textures of mince, zucchini and rice.

Preparation and marination **7 hours**
Cooking **20 minutes**

Meat with fat ground three times	750 g
Meat without fat hand minced	250 g

Marinade 1

Raw papaya paste	3 tbsp
Raw mango powder	1 tbsp
Green chillies minced	1 tbsp
Green coriander minced	2 tbsp
Cumin roasted and ground	2 tsp
Basil (sweet) minced	1/2 tbsp
Oil	2 tbsp

Marinade 2

Boiled rice*	1½ cup
Zucchini skinned sliced fine	1 cup
Green coriander chopped	2 tbsp
Egg	1
Salt	2 tsp
Oil for frying	as required
Food colour	optional

Basting

Oil	1/4 cup

Garnish
Mint yoghurt chutney
Peanut and cabbage relish

Mix the two minces and all ingredients of Marinade 1. Leave aside for six hours. Deep-fry the zucchini till all the water has evaporated. Put aside the eggs and add the zucchini to the other ingredients of Marinade 2. Run them through the blender and mix with the mince. The different textures should be distinctly visible. Beat the egg and add it to the mince mixture.

Oil and wipe the skewers. Press mince into sausage-shaped kababs directly onto the skewers. Put the skewers in the tandoor and cook for ten minutes. Remove and stand upright against tandoor to let the drippings fall for about five minutes. Baste the kababs and put the skewers back in the tandoor for five minutes. When ready, garnish and serve.

* Long-grained basmati should not be used as it does not have much binding power. Any glutinous rice is best for this recipe.

Leaf -Wrapped Kabab

*As the name suggests, this is a kabab wrapped in a leaf,
giving it an unusually attractive look. Banana leaf is the ideal
choice, but cabbage leaves will do just as well.*

Preparation and marination **7 hours**
Cooking **20 minutes**

Banana leaves 8" long or	
large cabbage leaves	8
Mince hand-chopped	500 g
Split chickpea	1/2 cup

Marinade

Lemon juice	3 tbsp
Ginger grated	1 tsp
Green chillies chopped	3
Green coriander chopped	1 tbsp
Black pepper powder	1 tsp
Curry masala	2 tsp
Oil	2 tbsp
Salt	1 tsp

Basting

Oil	1/4 cup

Garnish

Gherkin dil pickle
Mustard chutney

Soak the split chickpeas in water overnight. Mix all ingredients of the marinade other than the salt, and add to the mince. Leave aside for six hours. Boil the split chickpeas for ten minutes. Drain, grind and add to the mince. Now add the salt and steam the mince for ten minutes. Cool and grind this mince mixture.

Divide the mince into eight medium sized kababs (approx). Baste these kababs. Oil the banana leaves and wrap one kabab to one leaf. Make the final product look like a package. Tie each with a string.

Suspend these packages on a hook and chain arrangement* into the tandoor and cook for twenty minutes. Usually this amount of time is enough to cook the mince but let your 'nose' be the best judge. When you get the meaty aroma of a well-done kabab, you will know is ready. Garnish and serve.

*   See The Final Stage

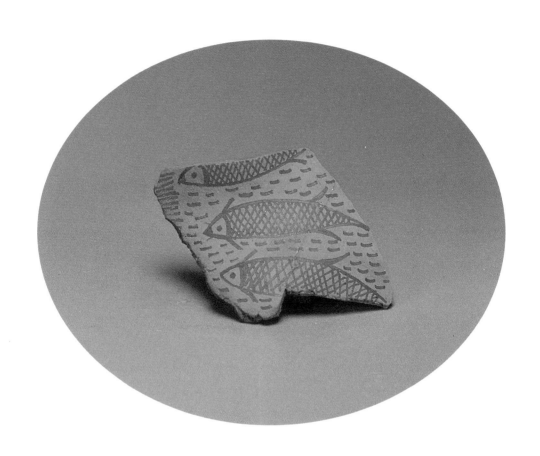

Fish

 In ancient times fish provided a rich source of proteins. Man is thought to have caught, prepared and eaten fresh and marine-water fish much before he domesticated animals. Today, of course, fish is an important part of most kitchens of the world.

In the *Arabian Nights* a number stories of exist about fish bones and how lethal they can be. Solutions given, such as boiling the fish till the bones dissolved, while they seem right in fiction, are not practical. If one was to resort to such techniques there would be no fish left to eat ! However, fish bones are never a problem to an experienced cook.

Nearly 1800 varieties of edible sea and fresh-water fish are known in India; singhara, salmon, sole, mali, surmai, rahu, pomfret and bhetki being the ones used most often in the Indian kitchens. Fish has very little fat and a high water content. This results in very delicate meat. Cooking time should be kept to a minimum as the fish tends to dry out if overcooked. It is for this reason that fish cooked in the tandoor is just perfect. The temperature remains low while the tandoor provides all-round heat for cooking the fish to just the 'right texture'. Basting should be done a couple of times to keep the fish moist. But keep an eye on the fish while it is cooking ! The cooking time is dictated by the type of cut you are using; and not by the length of the fish.

The type of cuts we use in the tandoor are:

Whole fish	Medium sized pomfret gives the best results.
Tikka	These are usually 2 to 2½ inch boneless pieces.
Mince	Fresh mince can be made, but in tandoori recipes the best results are obtained from steamed fish mince. Methods are described in individual recipes.

A word of advice here — deodorizing and skewering the fish in the correct way are the two most important features when cooking any of the following recipes. While skewering a whole fish, the skewer should pass along the backbone and parallel to it. Inserted at the mouth, it should emerge at the tail, without puncturing the fish at any other point. If skewered like this there is less chance of the fish slipping during cooking. It also improves the final presentation.

Marinades for whole fish can be used successfully for fish tikkas as well. Other sea-food is not often cooked in the tandoor, but tandoori prawns are very popular and I have included this recipe in the fish section.

Tikka and mince

Prawns

183

Ajwaini Machhi

*Renowned all over India as an aid to digestion, ajwain (carum)
enhances the subtle flavour of whichever fish it is used with. The best
fish for this recipe would be singhara, small rahu or river salmon.
If these are not available pomfret always gives good results.*

Preparation and marination **4 hours**
Cooking **15 minutes**

Small fish	500 g
Deodorizing	
Lemon juice	3 tbsp
Water to cover fish	
Marinade	
Yoghurt	1 cup
Ginger paste	2 tbsp
Garlic paste	1 tbsp
Onion paste	1/4 cup
Green mint paste	1 tbsp
Green coriander paste	2 tbsp
Kharasani ajwain masala*	2 tsp
Red chilli powder	2 tsp
Turmeric powder	1 tsp
Raw mango powder	1 tsp
Oil	1/4 cup
Salt	1 tsp
Basting	
Oil	1/4 cup
Garnish	
Carum ground	
Lemon	
Peanut and cabbage relish	

Clean the fish. Remove the fins
and scales and soak in the deodorizing
ingredients for half an hour. Drain and
wash gently. Pat dry and score the fish.
Mix all the ingredients of the marinade
and pour the marinade on the fish.
Leave aside for three hours.

Oil and wipe the skewer. Skewer
the fish and baste it well with leftover
marinade. Put the skewer into the
tandoor and cook for five minutes.
Remove and stand upright against the
tandoor to let the drippings fall for
about five minutes. Baste and put the
skewer back in the tandoor for five
minutes. When ready, garnish
and serve.

*   See Basic Preparations.

Tandoori Masala Pomfret

This recipe is always a favourite wherever tandoori food is relished, and specially in North India. The selection of the type of fish is very important. In India, pomfret, a fairly delicate fish, is used, for which small brill may be substituted if required.

Preparation and marination **3 ½ hours**
Cooking **15 minutes**

Pomfret	500 g
Deodorizing	
Lemon juice	1 tbsp
Water	5 cups
Marinade	
Yoghurt	1 cup
Ginger paste	2 tbsp
Garlic paste	1 tbsp
Onion paste	1 tbsp
Black pepper ground	1 tsp
Garam masala	2 tsp
Red chilli powder	2 tsp
Cumin roasted and ground	1 tsp
Green coriander minced	1 tbsp
Oil	1/4 cup
Salt	1 tsp
Food colour	1 tsp
Basting	
Oil	1/4 cup
Lemon juice	1 tbsp
Garnish	
Tandoori khatta masala	
Mint yoghurt chutney	

Clean the fish. Remove the fins and scales and soak in the deodorizing ingredients for half an hour. Drain and wash gently. Pat dry and score the fish. Mix all the ingredients of the marinade and pour the marinade on the fish. Leave aside for three hours.

Oil and wipe the skewer. Skewer the fish and put the skewer into the tandoor and cook for five minutes. Remove and stand upright against tandoor to let the drippings fall for about five minutes. Baste and put back into the tandoor for five minutes. When ready, garnish and serve.

Recipe photograph overleaf

Khatti Meethi Machhi

*A sweet and sour fish, another South Indian style recipe
that could start your mouth watering.*

Preparation and marination **4 ½ hours**
Cooking **15 minutes**

Pomfret	500 g
Deodorizing stage 1	
Lemon juice	1 tbsp
Water	3 cups
Deodorizing stage 2	
Lemon juice	1 tbsp
Black pepper ground	1 tsp
Salt	1 tsp
Marinade	
Onion minced	1/2 cup
Ginger paste	1 tbsp
Green chillies minced	1 tbsp
Curry leaves minced	1 tbsp
Curry masala*	1 tbsp
Tamarind pulp	3 tbsp
Sugar	3 tbsp
Oil	3 tbsp
Salt	1 tsp
Food colour	1 tsp
Basting	
Oil	2 tbsp
Garnish	
Salt	
Black pepper powder	
Lemon	
Til chutney	

Clean the fish. Remove the fins and scales and soak in the first stage deodorizing ingredients for fifteen minutes. Drain and soak for half an hour in the second stage deodorizing ingredients. Drain and wash gently. Pat dry and score fish.

In a heavy-bottom pan put the oil of the marinade. When it is hot add the onion, ginger, green chillies and curry leaves. Stir fry till the onions are light brown. Add the curry masala and stir for a minute, add the tamarind pulp, sugar and salt. Cook for another five minutes. Remove, cool and run through the blender once. You should have a smooth thick marinade sauce. Pour the marinade over the fish. Leave aside for three hours.

Oil and wipe the skewer and skewer the fish. Put the skewer into the tandoor and cook for five minutes. Remove and stand upright to let the drippings fall for about five minutes. Baste and put the skewer back into the tandoor for about five minutes. When ready, garnish and serve.

*   See Basic Preparation

Machhi Seekh Kabab

Mustard oil has been used in cooking since Harappan times. Strangely, Bengal at the eastern end of India cooks in mustard oil even today. I wonder how the influence travelled from the west to the east.

Preparation and marination **1 ½ hours**
Cooking **10 minutes**

Bhetki fillets	1 kg
Deodorizing stage 1	
Lemon juice	1/4 cup
Salt	1 tsp
Deodorizing stage 2	
Mustard oil	2 tbsp
Split chickpea flour	1 cup
For steaming	
Garlic cloves minced	4
Salt	1 tsp
Marinade	
Ginger grated fine	2 tbsp
Green coriander minced	1/2 cup
Green chillies minced	6
Roasted Bengal gram-flour	1 cup
Turmeric powder	1/2 tsp
Black pepper	1 tbsp
Mustard oil	1/4 cups
Salt	2 tsp
Basting	
Oil	2 tbsp

Garnish
Coriander powder
Raw mango powder
White radish relish

Rub the fish with the deodorizing ingredients for stage 1 and keeping aside for thirty minutes. Wash and dry the fish. Rub the second stage ingredients on and keep aside for another thirty minutes. Then, wash the fish and sprinkle with minced garlic cloves and salt and steam for ten minutes. When the fish is tender remove the bones. Mash it coarsely. Add all the ingredients of the marinade and mix to a well-blended uniform consistency.

Oil and wipe the skewers. Press into sausage-shaped kababs directly onto the skewers. Baste and put into the tandoor and cook for five minutes. These kababs take very little time, between five and ten minutes to cook. Check once after the first five minutes. When ready, garnish and serve.

Mung Machhi Seekh

This recipe is for the calorie conscious. It is rich in protein and fantastically low on fat.

Preparation and marination **3 hours**
Cooking **15 minutes**

Bhetki fillets	1 kg
Sprouted green lentil	1 cup
Water	1 cup
Salt	1/2 tsp
Deodorizing stage 1	
Chickpea flour	1 cup
Deodorizing stage 2	
Lemon juice	1/4 cup
Marinade 1	
Ginger grated fine	2 tsp
Spring onions minced	2
Green chillies minced	6
Green coriander minced	2 tbsp
Turmeric powder	1 tsp
Cumin roasted and ground	1 tsp
Raw mango powder	1 tsp
Oil	1/4 cup
Salt	1 tsp
Marinade 2	
Corn flour	3 tbsp
Eggs	2
Basting	
Oil	1/4 cup
Garnish	
Zeerawala namak	
Lemon	
Cucumber relish	

Wash the fish thoroughly. Rub with deodorizing stage 1 ingredients and leave aside for fifteen minutes. Wash and dry. Rub with the second stage ingredients and leave aside for one hour. Wash and dry. Steam the fish for ten minutes. When the fish is tender, remove the bones and mash coarsely.

Mix the ingredients of Marinade 1 with the mashed fish and leave aside for one hour. Put the sprouts in water with the salt and boil, making sure not to over-boil. Drain and mash coarsely. Beat the eggs, add the corn flour, mix and blend with the fish. Add the mashed sprouts and make a uniform mix.

Oil and wipe the skewers. Press into sausage-shaped kababs directly onto the skewers. Put the skewers into the tandoor and cook for five minutes. Remove and baste. Put the skewers back into the tandoor for five minutes. When ready, garnish and serve.

Malai Machhi Tikka

*Singhara, mali or surmai are perfect for this recipe. Effective
deodorizing is critical to achieve the subtle flavour of this recipe.*

Preparation and marination **4 ½ hours**
Cooking **15 minutes**

Singhara tikka	1 kg
Deodorizing stage 1	
Salt	2 tsp
Deodorizing stage 2	
Chickpea flour	1 cup
Deodorizing Stage 3	
Lemon juice	1/4 cup
Garlic paste	2 tsp
Marinade	
Oil	1/2 cup
Onions chopped	2
Yoghurt	1 cup
Ginger paste	2 tsp
Garlic paste	1 tsp
Cumin roasted and ground	1 tsp
Red chilli powder	1 tbsp
Fenugreek seed roasted and ground	1/2 tsp
Raw mango powder	2 tsp
Roasted gram-flour	1 cup
Double cream	1/2 cup
Salt	2 tsp
Food colour	1 tsp
Egg yolks	2
Basting	
Oil	1/4 cup
Garnish	
Green coriander chutney	

Rub the fish tikkas thoroughly with the deodorizing ingredients of stage 1 and wash. Repeat with stage 2 deodorizer and keep for half an hour. Mix the lemon juice and garlic paste (deodorizer stage 3) and put the tikkas in this for one hour. Drain, wash gently and dry.

Heat the oil for the marinade and fry the onions in this till golden brown. Cool and grind the onions. Mix these with the rest of the ingredients of the marinade apart from the yolks. Make a smooth thick marinade. Put the fish tikkas in this. Leave aside for two hours. Beat the egg yolks and mix them into the marinated tikkas. Blend in well.

Oil and wipe the skewers. Skewer the tikkas. Baste with leftover marinade and put the skewers into the tandoor and cook for five minutes. Remove and stand upright against tandoor to let the drippings fall for about five minutes. Baste and put the skewers back into the tandoor for five minutes. When ready, garnish and serve.

Tandoori Jhinga

For prawn lovers here is the ultimate delight. Can be served well-coated with or without crisp batter.

Preparation and marination **5 hours**
Cooking **15 minutes**

King prawns	25
Deodorizing	
Chickpea flour	1 cup
Marinade	
Yoghurt	1 cup
Hung yoghurt	1/2 cup
Lemon juice	2 tbsp
Ginger paste	1 tbsp
Onion paste	3 tbsp
Garam masala	2 tsp
Red chilli powder	2 tsp
Green coriander minced	2 tbsp
Green mint leaves minced	1 tsp
Oil	1/4 cup
Salt	1 tsp
Batter	
Cream	2 tbsp
Yoghurt	1/2 cup
Flour	3 tbsp
Eggs	2
Salt	1 tsp
Basting	
Oil	1/4 cup

Garnish
Tandoori khatta masala
Lemon
Mint yoghurt chutney

Shell and de-vein the prawns. Rub the deodorizing ingredients. Leave aside for half an hour. Wash, drain and pat dry. Mix all the ingredients of the marinade and put the prawns in this. Leave aside for four hours.

Mix all the ingredients of the batter and blend well. Dip prawns one at a time to coat them with the batter.

Oil and wipe the skewers. Skewer the prawns as you dip them in the batter one by one till all the skewers are ready. Put them into the tandoor and cook for five minutes. Remove the skewers and stand upright against tandoor to let the drippings fall for about five minutes. Baste and put the skewers back into the tandoor for five minutes. When ready, garnish and serve.

Where batter is not required the prawns can be skewered and cooked after the four-hour marination stage.

Vegetables

 We in India are lucky to have fresh vegetables all the year round. Availability is not the only advantage, we enjoy the luxury of the goods being delivered to our doorstep by our own sabziwala. He is the special man the ladies wait for to bring their daily supply of fresh vegetables.

The best vegetarian kitchens are in the Jain and Buddhist areas like Gujarat in Western India, and the Udipi kitchen of South India which is one of the finest examples of wholesome and healthy vegetarian food. Kayasth kitchens, both vegetarian and non-vegetarian, were already in existence before the age of the Mughals.

The kitchens of the Mughal kings could be compared to those of the Chinese rulers. Just as every ruler in Peking had to be impressed, in Northern India, every Mughal King had to be impressed. The Mughals patronized the Kayasth cuisine and many new recipes were known by the name of the patron, not by the name of the chef who created them. In other words patronage gave the names to various styles of cooking in those times.

As far as vegetarian tandoori or barbecued foods are concerned, they really achieved recognition very recently. Most recipes given here are my own innovations. The permutations and combinations are limitless. I have given as wide a range of recipes as possible.

Vegetables when cooked in the tandoor retain most of their food value as the juices are sealed within by the high temperatures and limited cooking time. According to me this concept opens up a whole new world in tandoori cuisine.

The section has been broadly divided and catagorized for convenience into:

Whole vegetables	As in tandoori alu.
Whole stuffed	These are whole vegetables with stuffings.
Tikka	Vegetables or Indian cottage cheese made into two inch cubes or as in the mixed seekhs.
Mince	These are recipes that use mashed vegetables.

Tandoori Gobi

Gobi or cauliflower is a vegetable that lends itself to any,
be it the Indian or the Western, kitchen. It is available and eaten
across the world, boiled, baked, sauted, grilled, curried and
cooked in the tandoor!

Preparation and marination 1 ½ hours
Cooking 15 minutes

Large cauliflowers	2
Marinade	
Ginger paste	1 tbsp
Garlic paste	2 tsp
Carum	1/2 tsp
Red chilli powder	2 tsp
Yoghurt	1 cup
Split chickpea flour	1 cup
Oil	3 tbsp
Salt	2 tsp
Food colour	1 tsp
Basting	
Oil	3 tbsp
Garnish	
Kharasani ajwain masala	
Peanut chutney	
Onion tomato yoghurt salad	

Cut the cauliflower into medium-sized florets, leaving inch long stalks for easy skewering.

Prick the florets lightly all over. Mix all ingredients of the marinade to a uniform thick consistency. Put the florets in the marinade for one hour, turning at regular intervals.

Oil and wipe the skewers. Skewer the cauliflower florets. Make sure they are well covered with the marinade. Put the skewers into the tandoor and cook for five minutes. Remove the skewers and baste. Put them back into the tandoor for a couple of minutes. When ready, garnish and serve.

Tandoori Alu

The humble potato is the most wholesome, versatile and adaptable food on earth. Having travelled around the world in the sixteenth and seventeenth century, it has had its ups and downs. Today the potato is here to stay.

Preparation and marination **1 hour**
Cooking **10 minutes**

Potatoes large (with skin)	8
Basting	
Butter	1/4 cup
Garnish	
Butter	3/4 cup
Green chillies minced	10
Lemon	
Zeerawala namak	

Oil and wipe the skewers. Skewer the potatoes through the longer plane. Baste lightly with butter and put the skewers into the tandoor and cook for five minutes. Remove the skewers and baste again. Put them back into the tandoor for five minutes. When ready take out the whole potatoes on a plate. Cut them lengthwise into halves. Score the pulp and put a teaspoonful of butter on each half. Mash in slightly with a fork. Add some minced green chillies, sprinkle zeerawala namak and squeeze the lemon on top. Serve as hot as possible.

Tandoori Eggs

This recipe is ideal in combination with various types of kababs served as a light snack in the evening.

Preparation and marination **2 hours**
Cooking **10 minutes**

Hard boiled eggs	6
Small potatoes	8

Stuffing

Spring onions minced	1/2 cup
Garlic paste	1 tsp
Black pepper ground	2 tsp
Elaichi jaiphal masala	1 tsp
Salt	1 tsp

Batter

Split chickpea flour	2 cups
Yoghurt	2 tbsp
Red chilli powder	2 tsp
Elaichi jaiphal masala	1/2 tsp
Salt	1 tsp
Water to make a thick batter	

Basting

Oil	2 tbsp

Garnish

Chilli garlic chutney
Cucumber relish

Cut the eggs in half and remove the yolks. Mix the yolks with stuffing ingredients and blend well with a fork. Fill the eggs with this mix, close the halves and tie with some kitchen string.

Mix ingredients for the batter. This should be thick enough to coat the eggs well. Put the eggs into this batter and leave aside for one hour.

Oil and wipe the skewers. Skewer the eggs perpendicular to the plane cut. Skewer a potato in between each egg to prevent it from slipping. Put the skewers into the tandoor and cook for five minutes. Remove the skewers and baste the eggs. Put the skewers back into the tandoor for five minutes. When they are golden brown, garnish and serve.

Tandoori Alu Bharwan

*The greatest thing about potatoes is that whichever way
you treat them, they always give good results.*

Preparation and marination   **1 ½ hours**
Cooking **10 minutes**

Potatoes large	8
Oil for deep frying	

Stuffing

White button mushrooms	
minced	2 cups
Onions minced	2
Tomatoes minced	2

Marinade

Yoghurt	1/2 cup
Ginger paste	2 tsp
Garlic paste	1 tsp
Green chillies minced	8
Green coriander minced	2 tbsp
Aromatic garam masala	1 tsp
Vegetarian stock cubes	2
Salt	2 tsp

Basting

Oil	2 tbsp

Garnish

Green coriander chutney
Cucumber relish

Deep fry the potatoes with skin in hot oil for eight to ten minutes. Drain and let them cool. Cut off a circle from the longer end. Keep aside. Gently scoop out the flesh to within half an inch of the skin.

Wash and drain the mushrooms. Mix all the ingredients of the marinade and soak the stuffing in this for one hour. In a heavy bottom pan cook the mushrooms and marinade mix over a slow fire. Cook till dry and oil is released. Drain the oil. Carefully fill all the potatoes with the mixture and close the caps. Tie with a kitchen string.

Oil and wipe the skewers. Skewer the potatoes through the cap. Small onions may be used to prevent the potatoes from slipping. Baste and put the skewers into the tandoor and cook for ten minutes. When ready, cut in half, garnish and serve.

Baigan Sabji Wala

Round baigans (brinjals), because of their natural shape
are very good for stuffing. This recipe is one of my favourites.

Preparation and marination **2 hours**
Cooking **10 minutes**

Large round brinjals	3

Marinade

Lemon juice	1/2 cup
Black pepper ground	1 tsp
Salt	1 tsp

Stuffing

Potatoes diced or	
peas shelled	1 cup
Onions large chopped	2
Tomatoes large chopped	2
Ginger paste	2 tsp
Garlic paste	1 tsp
Green chillies chopped	3
Red chilli powder	1 tsp
Cumin seed	1 tsp
Turmeric powder	1/2 tsp
Pomegranate ground	2 tsp
Yoghurt	1/2 cup
Oil	1/4 cup
Salt	2 tsp

Basting

Oil	2 tbsp

Garnish

Raw mango powder
Mustard chutney
White radish relish

Mix all the ingredients of the marinade. Cut the tops of the brinjals and scoop out the pulp to within three quarters of an inch of the skin. Apply marinade to the inside and outside of the brinjals. Leave aside for half an hour.

In the meantime heat the oil, add the cumin, onions, ginger and garlic paste. Stir fry till glazed. Add pulp of the brinjals and the rest of the ingredients apart from the yoghurt. Cook the whole mixture well, adding yoghurt at regular intervals. Cool and drain the excess oil.

Fill the brinjals with this mix, close with the caps. Tie them up with a kitchen string.

Oil and wipe the skewers. Skewer the brinjals. Put the skewers into the tandoor and cook for five minutes. Remove the skewers and baste. Put them back into the tandoor for five minutes or till the aroma is irresistible. When ready, garnish and serve.

Tamatar Baigan Wale

Stuffed tomatoes are irresistible, both to the eye and to the palate.
They make excellent starters to any meal.

Preparation and marination 2 hours
Cooking 10 minutes

Large firm red tomatoes	6
Stuffing	
Whole large brinjal	1
Onions minced	2
Tomatoes minced	2
Green chillies minced	6
Cumin seeds	1 tsp
Coriander roasted and ground	2 tsp
Green coriander minced	1 tbsp
Oil	3 tbsp
Salt	1 tsp
Batter	
Eggs	2
Split chickpea flour	1/2 cup
Double cream	1/2 cup
Coriander powder	1 tsp
Salt	1 tsp
Garnish	
Besan til masala	

Singe the brinjal—when the tandoor is lit you can skewer it whole with the skin and singe in the tandoor. Alternately singe on the gas or in the oven. Immerse in water and remove the skin. Beat the pulp in a chopping motion till nicely pulped.

Heat oil in a heavy bottom pan. Put in the cumin. When it splutters, put in the rest of the stuffing ingredients apart from the tomatoes. Add the pulped brinjal. Stir fry well. Add the tomatoes and cook till the mixture leaves oil*. Drain excess oil and put aside.

Wash and dry the whole tomatoes. Cut off the top and scoop out the pulp carefully. Fill in the brinjal mixture, close the top and tie with some kitchen string.

Beat the eggs and mix with the split chickpea flour, cream and salt. Coat the tomatoes with this batter.

Oil and wipe the skewers. Skewer the tomatoes. Small onions or halved potatoes may be used to prevent the tomatoes from slipping. Put the skewers into the tandoor and cook till the batter is golden brown. Garnish and serve.

*   This is the baigan bharta preparation.

Ingredients for the batter

Simla mirch with both the alu and chane ki dal stuffing. Shown here before cooking and on the facing page after cooking in the tandoor.

Simla Mirch Alu Wali

*Usually highly underestimated, the simla mirch or capsicum
is used in many ways in the Indian kitchen.*

Preparation and marination **1 ½ hours**
Cooking **10 minutes**

Capsicum large size	8

Marinade

Lemon juice	1/2 cup
Ginger paste	1 tsp
Garlic paste	1/2 tsp
Oil	3 tbsp
Salt	1 tsp

Stuffing

Potatoes diced small	5
Green coriander chopped	1 tbsp
Panch phoran masala*	1 tbsp
Turmeric powder	1 tsp
Red chilli powder	1 tsp
Asfoetida (compounded) powder	1/4 tsp
Oil	2tbsp
Salt	1 tsp

Basting

Oil	2 tbsp

Garnish
Mixed vegetable pickle

Cut the caps of the capsicum. Remove the seeds. Mix all the ingredients of the marinade and rub liberally on the insides of the capsicums. Cover with caps and leave aside for one hour.

Peel and dice the potatoes (to pea size). Wash and drain. Take a heavy bottom pan and heat the oil. Put in the panch phoran masala. As it splutters, put in the rest of the stuffing ingredients. Cook till potatoes turn golden. Drain the oil and cool. Stuff the capsicums with these potatoes. They should be stuffed well but not to bursting point. Cover with the caps and tie them with some kitchen string.

Oil and wipe the skewers. Skewer the capsicums. Small onions or pieces of potatoes can be used to prevent them from slipping. Baste and put the skewers into the tandoor and cook for five minutes. Remove the skewers, baste and put back into the tandoor for a couple of minutes. Garnish and serve.

*   See glossary of names.

Recipe photographs on previous pages

Simla Mirch aur Chane Ki Dal

Capsicum and chana dal (split chickpea) make an interesting combination. The spicier the dish the tastier it will be.

Preparation and marination **2 hours**
Cooking **10 minutes**

Capsicums large size	8
Marinade	
Lemon juice	1/2 cup
Oil	1 tsp
Cumin roasted and ground	1 tsp
Salt	1 tsp
Stuffing	
Split chickpea	1 cup
Water	1 cup
Onions minced	1/2 cup
Green chillies minced	2 tsp
Green coriander minced	2 tbsp
Red chilli powder	1 tsp
Turmeric powder	1 tsp
Cumin seeds	1/2 tsp
Raw mango powder	1 tsp
Oil	1 tbsp
Salt	1 tsp
Basting	
Oil	2 tbsp

Garnish
Onion tomato yoghurt salad

Cut the caps of the capsicums. Remove the seeds. Mix all the ingredients of the marinade and rub liberally on the inside. Leave aside for one hour. Soak the split chickpeas for half an hour. Then boil in one cup of water till the water dries up. Heat the oil in a heavy bottom pan; add all the stuffing ingredients. Stir a minute, then add the split chickpeas and stir fry for five minutes. No water should be added and any excess oil should be drained off. Fill each capsicum with this mixture. Cover with the caps and tie with kitchen string.

Oil and wipe the skewers. Skewer the capsicum through the cap and put the skewers into the tandoor and cook for five minutes. Remove and baste lightly with oil. Put the skewers back into the tandoor for couple of minutes. When ready, garnish and serve.

Recipe photograph on pages 212 and 213

Tandoori Ghia

The round gourd is a seasonal vegetable. The flesh is white and the ones we use here are small and tender. It does not have any flavour on its own, but put in curries, fried with masalas or stuffed as in this recipe, it is delicious.

Preparation and marination **2 hours**
Cooking **15 minutes**

Whole round gourds	3

Marinade

Lemon juice	1/2 cup
Red chilli powder	2 tsp
Garam masala	2 tsp
Salt	1 tsp

Stuffing

Indian cottage cheese loose	1 cup
Onions minced	1/2
Tomatoes minced	1/2 cup
Green chillies minced	1 tbsp
Ginger grated	2 tsp
Garlic grated	1 tsp
Green coriander minced	1 tbsp
Cumin seeds	1/2 tsp
Oil	2 tbsp
Salt	1 tsp

Basting

Oil	2 tbsp

Garnish

Green coriander chutney

Single boil the gourds. Cut the caps and scoop out the flesh to within three-quarters of an inch of the skin. Score the inside and outside surface lightly. Mix all the ingredients of the marinade. Rub this all over the inside and outside. Leave aside for one hour.

Heat the oil in a heavy bottom pan. Add the cumin. When it splutters add the rest of the stuffing ingredients apart from the cottage cheese and salt. Stir these till they are fairly well cooked. Add the cottage cheese and the salt and mix well. Cool and drain any excess oil. Stuff the gourds. Cover the tops with the caps and tie securely with some kitchen string.

Oil and wipe the skewers. Skewer the gourds. While skewering it is better to have one gourd to one skewer and use a potato at the base to prevent it from slipping. Put the skewers into the tandoor and cook for five minutes. Remove the skewers and baste. Put back into the tandoor for five minutes. When ready, garnish and serve.

Tandoori Baigan Tikka

*I have often wondered why many more vegetables are not
cooked in the tandoor. The tandoor imparts a unique flavour,
and if they are properly marinated — it is fat free cooking!*

Preparation and marination **3 hours**
Cooking **10 minutes**

Brinjal tikka	3
Small onions	20

Marinade

Yoghurt	1 cup
Vinegar	1 tbsp
Ginger paste	1 tbsp
Garlic paste	2 tsp
Onion paste	2 tbsp
Fenugreek green leaves chopped	1 tbsp
Garam masala	1 tsp
Cumin powder	1 tsp
Red chilli powder	2 tsp
Oil	2 tbsp
Salt	2 tsp
Food colour	1 tsp

Basting
Leftover marinade

Garnish
Til chutney
Onion rings
Lemon

Mix all the ingredients of the marinade. Prick and soak the tikkas in this for two hours.

Oil and wipe the skewers. Skewer the tikkas with small onions between them to prevent them from slipping. Baste well with the leftover marinade. Put the skewers into the tandoor and cook for five minutes. Remove and baste again. Put them back into the tandoor for a couple of minutes. When ready, garnish and serve. The small onions can be eaten as well.

Bewazni Panir Tikka

*This panir is literally weightless. The technique for making
it is not easily or often disclosed.*

Preparation and marination **2 ½ hours**
Cooking **10 minutes**

Indian cottage cheese tikka*	12
Water to cover tikka	

Marinade 1

Lemon juice	1/2 cup
Red chilli powder	2 tsp
Cumin roasted and ground	1 tsp
Salt	1 tsp

Marinade 2

Yoghurt	1/2 cup
Ginger paste	2 tbsp
Green chilli paste	1 tbsp
Black pepper powder	1 tsp
Carum seed	1/2 tsp
Caraway seed	1/2 tsp
Turmeric powder	1/2 tsp
Split chickpea flour	1/2 cup
Salt	1 tsp
Red colour	optional

Basting

Oil	1/4 cup

Garnish

Tandoori khatta masala
Lemon
Cachumbar relish
Mixed vegetable pickle

Put the cottage cheese tikkas in a pan
and cover them with water, set to boil.
When they rise and float to the top,
drain and cool. Mix all the ingredients
of Marinade 1. Coat the tikkas with
this mix while turning by hand. Leave
aside for one hour. Mix all ingredients
of Marinade 2 and put the tikkas in it.
Leave aside for one hour.

Oil and wipe the skewers. Skewer the
tikkas. Put the skewers into the tandoor
and cook for five minutes. Remove the
skewers, baste and put back for two
or three minutes. When ready, garnish
and serve.

* See Basic Preparation

Hari Seekh

Roasted greens have a unique flavour and can be served with any meat dish.

Preparation and marination **2 hours**
Cooking **10 minutes**

Broad-beans	20
Spinach leaves (no stem)	20
Broccoli (medium florets)	20
Spring onions (without leaves)	10
Cabbage (medium)	1

Marinade

Yoghurt	2 cups
Onion paste	1/4 cup
Black pepper ground	2 tbsp
Garam masala	2 tsp
Raw mango powder	1/2 tsp
Peanut oil	2 tbsp
Salt	2 tsp

Basting
Leftover marinade

Garnish
Tandoori khatta masala

Cut the broad-beans in half, remove the leaves of the cabbage. Clean and wash all the greens.

Mix all the ingredients of the marinade and put the vegtables in this. Leave aside for one hour, turning at regular intervals.

Oil and wipe the skewers. Skewer the greens in any order. The spinach and cabbage leaves have to be doubled while skewering for better results. Baste with leftover marinade and put the skewers into the tandoor and cook for two minutes. Remove the skewers and baste again. Put the skewers back into the tandoor for a couple of minutes. When ready, garnish and serve.

Mixed Seekh I

*One of the most popular vegetarian combinations served
with non-vegetarian tandoori or barbecued foods.*

Preparation and marination **2 hours**
Cooking   **10 minutes**

Indian cottage cheese tikka*	12
Whole cherry tomatoes	14
Whole small onions	14
Small capsicums**	6
Green coriander minced	1 tbsp
Green chillies minced	4
Cumin roasted and ground	1 tsp
Salt	1 tsp

Marinade

Yoghurt	2 cups
Black pepper ground	2 tsp
Red chilli powder	1 tsp
Garam masala	1 tsp
Oil	2 tbsp
Salt	1 tsp

Basting
Leftover marinade

Garnish
Tandoori khatta masala
Green coriander chutney

Prepare cottage cheese tikkas as in
Basic Preparation given on page 72. The
addition of coriander, chillies, cumin
and salt at the curdling stage will make
a spicy cottage cheese.

Wash and dry the vegetables. Mix
all the ingredients of the marinade and
soak the cottage cheese and all the
vegetables in the mix. Leave aside
for one hour.

Oil and wipe the skewers. Skewer
onion, tomato, capsicum and cottage
cheese tikkas alternately till all the
vegetables are used up. Baste and put
the skewers into the tandoor and cook
for five minutes. Remove the skewers
and baste again. Put the skewers back
into the tandoor for a couple of
minutes. When ready, garnish
and serve.

*   See Basic Preparations.

** In case small capsicums are not
    available large ones can be cut into
    pieces and used.

Mixed Seekh II

Another version of mixed seekhs making use of vegetables with pulp. These look the same, but taste so different.

Preparation and marination **1 ½ hours**
Cooking **10 minutes**

Potato tikka	5
Sweet potato tikka	3
Yam tikka 1½ inch square pieces	10
Raw banana tikka	3

For boiling

Khatti lassi	3 cups
Green chilli paste	1 tbsp
Salt	2 tsp

Marinade

Yoghurt	1 cup
Garam masala	2 tsp
Ginger paste	2 tbsp
Garlic paste	1 tbsp
Green mint minced	1tsp
Red chilli powder	2 tsp
Oil	1/4 cup
Salt	1 tsp
Food colour	1 tsp

Basting
Leftover marinade

Garnish
Tandoori khatta masala
Lemon
Mint yoghurt chutney

Mix the boiling ingredients and bring to a boil. Put in all the vegetable tikkas and boil till they are half-done. Drain and cool.

Mix all the ingredients of the marinade and put the vegetables in this so they are well coated. Leave aside for half an hour.

Oil and wipe the skewers. Skewer potato and, the sweet potato, followed by yam and raw banana alternately. Put the skewers into the tandoor and cook for five minutes. Remove the skewers and baste. Put them back into the tandoor for a couple of minutes. When ready, garnish and serve.

Alu Seekh Kabab

Potatoes have been used as fillers, binders and supporters. Here is a recipe that does justice to one of nature's most wondrous gifts !

Preparation and marination **1 hour**
Cooking **10 minutes**

Potatoes medium	5
French beans chopped fine	1/2 cup
Carrots chopped fine	1/2 cup
Ginger grated fine	1 tsp
Garlic chopped fine	1/2 tsp
Green chillies minced	2 tsp
Green coriander minced	2 tbsp
Raw mango powder	1 tsp
Garam masala	1 tsp
Bread crumbs	1/2 cup
Butter	1 tsp
Salt	1 tsp

Basting

Butter melted	2 tbsp

Garnish

Green coriander chutney
Zeerawala namak
Lemon

Boil the potatoes with skin. Cool and remove the skin. Mash the potatoes. Boil the beans and carrots in just enough water to soften the vegetables. Mix all other ingredients with the vegetables and knead into a dough.

Oil and wipe the skewers. Press into sausage-shaped kababs directly onto the skewers. Apply a gentle pressure while shaping kababs. Baste and put into the tandoor and cook till golden brown. Garnish and serve.

Overleaf: Alu Seekh, Vegetable Seekh, Corn Seekh, Tofu Seekh and Hare Chane ki Seekh.

Vegetable Seekh and Tomato Chutney

Alu Seekh and Coriander Chutney

Tofu Seekh and Til Chutney

*Corn Seekh
and
Mint Chutney*

*Hare Chane ka Seekh
and Pickled Onions*

Vegetable Seekh Kabab

Vegetables in India are plentiful, providing unlimited combinations for making vegetable seekh kababs. The recipe given below has proved to be very popular with all my friends.

Preparation and marination **1 hour**
Cooking **10 minutes**

Potatoes medium	4
Yam chopped	2 cups
Indian cottage cheese (loose)	1/2 cup
Cashewnuts ground	1/2 cup
Ginger paste	2 tsp
Garlic paste	1 tsp
Onion minced	1/2 cup
Green chillies minced	1 tbsp
Green coriander minced	2 tbsp
Cumin roasted	1 tsp
Red chilli powder	1 tsp
Bread crumbs	1 cup
Salt	2 tsp
Food colour	1 tsp

Basting

Oil	2 tbsp

Garnish

Tandoori khatta masala
Tomato chutney
White radish relish

Boil the potatoes and the yam separately. Mash them. Knead all the other ingredients with the potatoes and yam, making a slightly stiff dough.

Oil and wipe the skewers. Press into sausage-shaped kababs directly onto the skewers. Baste and put them into the tandoor and cook for about eight minutes or till golden brown.
Garnish and serve.

Corn Seekh Kabab

Corn (bhutta) is very popular in India. During peak season one can see bhuttas being roasted on makeshift angeethis at the corner of every street. Corn can be prepared in many ways. One novel way is the corn seekh kabab.

Preparation and marination **2 hours**
Cooking **10 minutes**

Corn on the cob	4
Potatoes	5
Spring onions minced	1/4 cup
Green chillies minced	1 tbsp
Onion large minced	3/4 cup
Corn flour	1/4 cup
Oil	2 tsp
Salt	1 tsp

Basting

Melted butter	3 tbsp

Garnish
Zeerewala namak
Lemon
Mixed green relish

Remove the leaves from the corn and boil for twenty minutes. Tender corn will make better kababs. Grate the corn when slightly cool or remove the kernel and run them through a wet grinder once*. Boil the potatoes; cool, peel and mash them. Mix the potatoes, corn and all other ingredients. Blend really well to a dough-like consistency.

Oil and wipe the skewers. Press into sausage-shaped kababs directly on to the skewers. Baste and put into the tandoor and cook till golden. Garnish and serve.

*   Do not add any water.

Tofu Seekh Kabab

I have already stressed the versatility and nutritive
value of beancurd*. In this recipe we see once again, how tofu
can be adapted.

Preparation and marination **3 hours**
Cooking **10 minutes**

Tofu (loose)	2 cups
Split chickpea	1/2 cup
Water	1 cup

Marinade

Ginger paste	2 tsp
Garlic paste	1 tsp
Onion paste	1 tbsp
Mushrooms minced fine	1 cup
Corn flour	1/4 cup
Salt	1½ tsp

Frying Ingredients

Red chilli whole crushed	1
Kharasani ajwain masala	1 tsp
Green coriander minced	1 tsp
Oil	2tsp

Basting

Oil	3 tbsp

Garnish

Kharasani ajwain masala
Lemon
Til chutney

Prepare the loose tofu˙. Boil the split chickpea in one cup of water till the water dries up. Mix all ingredients of the marinade with the chickpea. Leave aside for one hour. Pound this whole to a uniform consistency.

Heat two teaspoons of oil and add all the frying ingredients. Stir for a minute; add the pounded mixture and stir for about another two minutes or till the water dries up. Remove from the heat and cool. When this mixture has cooled mix the tofu. Knead till you have a well-blended dough**.

Oil and wipe the skewers. Press into sausage-shaped kababs directly onto the skewers. Baste and put them into the tandoor and cook for five minutes. Garnish and serve.

*   See Basic Preparation

** The mix to be skewered should be as dry as possible.

Hare Chane ki Seekh

In my family chholia (green gram), as it is, called is a hot favourite. All generations sit and indulge in a chholia-eating orgy — eating straight from the pod. This recipe is a family favourite too.

Preparation and marination **2 hours**
Cooking **10 minutes**

Green gram peeled	3 cups
Hung yoghurt	1/2 cup
Ginger paste	1 tbsp
Garlic paste	2 tsp
Onion minced	1/2 cup
Green chillies minced	1 tbsp
Green coriander minced	1 tbsp
Coconut grated fine	1 cup
Curry leaves minced	a few
Cumin seed	1 tsp
Split chickpea flour	1/2 cup
Oil	3 tbsp
Salt	2 tsp

Basting

Oil	1/4 cup

Garnish
Green mint chutney
Pickled onions

Heat the oil and add the cumin. Then add the onions, chillies, ginger, garlic, curry leaves and coriander. Stir for a minute or two. Add the green gram and salt. Cover and cook for five minutes. Add the coconut and yoghurt and stir till the water dries up. Cool and mash the mixture while adding the split chickpea flour.

Oil and wipe the skewers. Press into sausage-shaped kababs directly on to the skewers. Baste and put the skewers into the tandoor and cook for five minutes. Remove the skewers, baste again and put back into the tandoor for a couple of minutes. When ready, garnish and serve.

Breads

 Bread, the one factor that unites man ! Everywhere, in every country, every city and every home, bread is prepared and eaten in one way or another. If one sits down and tries to list the types and names of breads made, it would be quite interesting to see the variety.

Wheat is the base from which we get flour. According to archaeologists wheat existed long before man became domesticated. In fact, wheat is thought to have made man a homemaker. To cultivate wheat once he discovered its properties, he had to stay in one place. From then he has never looked back. Experimenting with what was a wild grass to the long-eared, tightly packed wheat stalk we know today.

Wheat has been excavated in the Indus valley. An Egyptian bakery has been found that dates back to about the same time as the Harappan civilization. Ground wheat was used for bread then as it is now, the only difference being that the grinding mill has developed so much technically that ground flour is now available in large quantities, enabling everyone to develop and cook bread in his own style.

The tandoor was used to bake wholewheat bread. Tandoori roti has been known for the last 5000 years in India. All baked breads are not Indian; on the other hand, fried breads like puri, paratha, bhatura, are Indian. We have, unfortunately, lost the touch of making other non-fried breads such as methi-ka-phulka, besan-ki-roti, bajre-ki-roti. In my recipes I have suggested variations keeping in mind this age-old tradition.

There are certain terms used while making breads. These are briefly listed here.

Gluten : This is a natural substance in the flour that has a bonding effect. Kneading catalyses the action of this plant protein, and this, in turn, makes the dough hold.

Sift : This is a sieving process used for all flours.

Knead : Kneading is the most important process for making breads. It involves a rocking motion of both hands. The dough is first pushed with the palm of the hand and then folded over with the fingers. This process gives 'air' to the dough and makes it lighter. Kneading helps distribute yeast in yeast doughs. It activates the plant protein gluten in wheat flour. A well-kneaded dough should be non-sticky. When kneading one should take special care not to pour all the water at one spot on the flour. This will make the dough lumpy and uneven. By sprinkling a little at a time and kneading simultaneously, one can blend the flour and water well.

Dough : It is a preparation of flour and water kneaded till it is soft and pliable. It is ready for use when it is not sticky any more. Different recipes require varying amounts of flour and water—these are given in the individual recipes.

Leavening agents : Those substances that help the dough to rise, thereby trapping air. Usually yeast, baking soda, baking powder are used. For many Indian breads, yoghurt is used to ferment the dough.

Khamir : Soured dough used for leavening other breads (khamiri roti).

Flour : This is the dry flour used while flattening the dough before putting it in the tandoor. It prevents the wet dough from sticking to the hands. A separate quantity should be kept aside before starting to make any bread.

Finishing : Applying ghee or butter on the bread, usually after the bread is baked, while it is still hot.

Tandoori Roti

*The simplest and most popular roti
eaten with kali dal and tandoori meats.
It is usually made of whole-wheat flour
but bajra (millet), makki (corn), moth
(fox gram) and besan (split chickpea
flour) are all popular in North India.
These can be mixed in the ratio of 1
(wheat flour) : 3 (of any other flour),
to give good results in the tandoor.*

Whole wheat flour	500 g
Water	1 cup
Ghee	to taste

Sieve the flour. Sprinkle the water
and knead well to a non-sticky dough.
Set aside for half an hour.

Knead again and make eight to ten
equal balls and flatten each with the
hand* to give approximately an eight
inch diameter. Place on a cushion,
moisten the side facing up and slap on
to the walls of the hot tandoor. When
it begins to brown and bubble, remove
with a pair of bread seekhs. Spread
a teaspoon of ghee and serve hot.

Makhni Roti

*A wholesome bread specially
to be enjoyed on a journey or a picnic.*

Whole wheat flour	500 g
Water	1 cup
Butter	1/4 cup
Black pepper pounded	2 tsp
Salt	1/2 tsp

Sieve the flour. Mix the salt, pepper,
and crumble the butter. Sprinkle the
water and knead well to a non-sticky
dough.

Knead again and make eight to ten
equal balls and flatten with the hand to
approximately an eight-inch diameter*.
Place on a cushion, moisten the side
facing up and slap it on to the walls
of the hot tandoor. When it begins to
brown and bubble, remove with a pair
of bread seekhs. Spread a teaspoon
of ghee and serve hot.

For children a special variation can
be made, using a-quarter cup of sugar,
instead of salt and pepper.

* Flattening the dough with the hand
is the traditional way. You may use
a rolling pin and platter in case the
hand technique is not convenient.

*Previous pages clockwise from right:
Tandoori rotis made of bajra, makki, moth,
besan and plain flour.*

Recipe photograph on facing page

Khamiri Roti

This leavened bread is really an acquired taste. There are a number of ways to make the dough 'khamira'. The first and simplest is to leave the ordinary dough in a warm place for twelve hours. (This is my favourite). Another method is to knead the dough with yoghurt water. Finally, to make it easier, any leavening agent such as baking powder can be added.

Whole wheat flour	500 g
Water from drained yoghurt	1/2 cup
Water	1/2 cup
Carum seeds	1/2 tsp
Red chilli powder	1 tsp
Salt	1/2 tsp

Sieve the flour. Mix in the carum, red chilli powder and salt. Sprinkle the yoghurt water and plain water, knead well to a non-sticky dough. Set aside for three hours in a warm place.

Knead again and make eight to ten equal balls. Flatten with the hand to approximately an eight-inch diameter. Place on a cushion and moisten the side facing up; slap on to the walls of the hot tandoor. When the roti is brown and slightly crisp, remove with a pair of bread seekhs. Spread a teaspoon of ghee and serve hot.

Tandoori Paratha

Making this layered and flaky paratha is a great art. The more layers there are the greater the master chef ! Any number of garnishes can be used on tandoori parathas. Sesame, poppy seeds, nigella seeds, chopped mint or coriander leaves or red chillies. These can be sprinkled on and lightly pressed into the flattened dough on the side which does not stick to the tandoor.

Whole wheat flour	500 g
Water	1 cup
Salt	1/2 tsp
Ghee	1/2 cup

Sieve the flour. Mix in half the ghee and the salt. Sprinkle water and knead well to a non-sticky dough. Set aside for one hour.

Knead again and make six to eight equal balls to approximately an eight-inch diameter. Lightly spread melted ghee. Pleat the dough lengthwise into one collected strip. Twist this strip and coil. Flatten this coiled dough. Place on a cushion, moisten the side facing up and slap on to the walls of the hot tandoor. When brown and flaky, remove with a pair of bread seekhs. Spread ghee and serve hot.

Panir ka Paratha

A great family favourite. This paratha gives the best results when the panir (Indian cottage cheese) is fresh and home-made.

Whole wheat flour	500 g
Indian cottage cheese (loose)	1 cup
Water as required	
Green coriander minced	1 tbsp
Cumin roasted and ground	1/2 tsp
Green chillies minced	1 tsp
Salt	1 tsp
Ghee	1/4 cup

Sieve the flour. Mix in the coriander, cumin, chillies and salt. Rub in the panir till the flour looks crumbly. Sprinkle water and knead well to a non-sticky dough. Set aside for one hour. In warm climatic conditions do not keep the dough for too long otherwise it will begin to ferment.

Knead the dough again and make six to eight equal balls. Flatten each and spread a little ghee. Follow the same method of folding as in the previous recipe. Flatten out again into a square. Place on a cushion, moisten the side facing up and slap on to the walls of the hot tandoor. When it is light brown, use a pair of bread seekhs to remove. Spread a little ghee and serve hot.

Methi ka Paratha

A popular preparation. I can clearly recall from my childhood, ladies meticulously plucking the green methi (fenugreek) leaves from their stems, and the aroma of these parathas baking.

Whole wheat flour	500 g
Water	1 cup
Fenugreek leaves chopped	2 tbsp
Cumin roasted and ground	1/2 tsp
Red chilli powder	1 tsp
Salt	1 tsp
Ghee	1/4 cup

Sieve the flour. Mix the fenugreek leaves, cumin, red chillies and salt. Sprinkle the water and knead well to a non-sticky dough. Cover and set aside till required.

Knead the dough again. Make six to eight equal balls. Flatten or roll out to approximately an eight-inch diameter. Lightly spread melted ghee and cut into a number of strips. Place these one on top of the other and coil. Again flatten this coiled dough to approximately an eight-inch diameter. Place on a cushion, moisten the side facing up and slap it onto the walls of the hot tandoor. When it is light brown and flaky, use a pair of bread seekhs and remove. Spread a little ghee and serve hot.

Overleaf tandoori, methi and panir paratha

Nan

A leavened bread of exquisite taste, thought to have originated in Persia. The tradition carries on in modern day Iran. A very good flour mixture for nan is half white flour and half fine semolina flour. It will make a 'khasta' nan.

White flour	500 g
Yoghurt	1/2 cup
Baking powder	1 tsp
Yeast	1 tsp
Egg	1
Oil	2 tbsp
Salt	1/2 tsp
Water as required	

Sieve the flour. Mix in the baking powder, yeast and salt. Beat the egg slightly, mix this into the flour along with the oil and yoghurt. Sprinkle the water and knead well to a smooth and pliable dough. Set aside for three hours. Knead and set aside for another hour. By now the dough should have risen to almost double its original size.

Make eight to ten equal balls. Flatten each to approximately an eight inch diameter. Place on a cushion and moisten the side facing up. Pull the dough gently at one corner to give it the traditional elongated shape. Slap it on to the walls of the hot tandoor. When it browns slightly and rises it is ready. Use a pair of bread seekhs and remove. Spread a little ghee if required and serve hot.

Facing page: Nan and nan chana dal.

Nan Chana Dal

Stuffed nans are really wholesome. I have deviated from the usual method of mashed fillings and have used chana dal (split chickpea) to stuff the nan. Other whole stuffings one can use are peas (pre-cooked), other lentils, lamb mince, panir minced and cauliflower chopped (pre-cooked). As always innovations are endless and you can make your own.

Split chickpea*	1¼ cup
Garam masala	2 tsp
Green chillies chopped	3
Raw mango powder	1 tsp
Oil	1 tbsp
Salt	1 tsp
Water	2 ½ cups
Dough as in previous recipe	

Soak the chana dal for about one hour. After washing thoroughly, boil with salt and water till the water evaporates and the dal has softened. This can be stored in the fridge till one is ready to use it in the nan. Half an hour before stuffing in the nan, heat the oil in a pan and add green chillies. When they sizzle add the dal. Stir for a minute, add garam masala and raw mango powder and fry for two to three minutes. When completely dry take off from the fire and cool.

Make a round ball with the nan dough, (previous recipe) flatten it out a little, put a tablespoon of dal in the centre and gently raising the sides enclose the dal with the dough. Once again, slowly press this ball into a flat circular shape and bake in the tandoor.

* If soaked split chickpea is one cup use two cups of water while boiling it. (1:2)

Kulcha

This bread resembles the Italian pizza base. It blends wonderfully well with both 'chole' as well as with 'chilli con carne.' What versatility !

White flour	500 g
Baking powder	1 tbsp
Salt	1 tsp
Sugar	1 tsp
Oil	2 tbsp
Lukewarm water	1 cup

Sieve the flour. Mix in all the dry ingredients. Sprinkle water and knead well to a smooth well-blended dough. Set aside for four hours.

Knead the dough again and make eight to ten equal balls. Flatten these to approximately a six inch diameter. Place on a cushion, moisten the side facing up and slap on to the walls of the hot tandoor. When it browns slightly and rises, remove with a pair of bread seekhs and serve hot.

Sheermal

Sheermal, meaning milk and substance, is exactly what this rich man's bread is made of.

White flour	500 g
Ghee	1/2 cup
Double cream	2 tbsp
Sugar	1 tsp
Baking powder	2 tsp
Salt	1 tsp
Saffron	1/4 tsp
Milk	1 cup
Caradamom green powdered	6
Finishing	
Saffron	1/4 tsp
Milk	1/4 cup

Sieve the flour. Mix the ghee, sugar, baking powder, salt, quarter teaspoon of saffron and cardamom into the flour. Sprinkle one cup of milk and knead well to make a soft dough. Set aside for half an hour.

Knead the dough again and make eight to ten equal sized balls. Flatten these to approximately a six inch diameter. Place on a cushion, moisten the side facing up and slap it onto the walls of the hot tandoor. When light brown, remove with a pair of bread seekhs. Soak 1/4 teaspoon saffron in a-quarter cup of milk. Brush the top of the hot sheermal with this milk to give it a very special flavour.

Khatta Masaledar Maza

Made with split chickpea flour curry, this is a hot and spicy treat.

Whole wheat flour	500 g
Yoghurt (soured)	1 cup
Split chickpea flour	1/2 cup
Turmeric powder	1 tsp
Cumin seeds	1/2 tsp
Fenugreek seeds	1/4 tsp
Red chilli powder	1 tsp
Ginger minced	1/2 tsp
Asafoetida	
(compounded powder)	1/4 tsp
Green coriander minced	1/4 tsp
Green chillies minced	1 tsp
Oil	1 tbsp
Salt	1/2 tsp
Water	2 cups

Beat the yoghurt, split chickpea flour, turmeric, red chillies, ginger, asafoetida, salt and water together. There should be no lumps in this mixture. In a heavy bottom vessel heat the oil and splutter the fenugreek and cumin seeds. Pour the yoghurt mixture, stirring continuously to avoid any lumps. When it begins to bubble, cook on a low flame till the mixture thickens. Add green coriander and green chillies. Cool.

Sieve the flour, knead with one cup of the cooled curry to make a well-blended non-sticky dough.

Make six to eight equal balls. Flatten each by hand to approximately an eight inch diameter. Place on a cushion, moisten the side facing up and slap onto the walls of the hot tandoor. When light brown, remove with a pair of bread seekhs. Spread a little ghee and serve hot.

Accompaniments

Chutneys are an essential part of the Indian kitchen. These tasty preparations add just the right finishing touch. Here, in the tandoori kitchen, they are important garnishes. Traditionally chutneys were ground on the grind stone or silbatta. The electronic era has brought in food processors, blenders, etc. Though the task becomes easier the flavour always loses out a bit.

A relish is the savoury bit that adds zest to the food. In my recipes these are a collection of fresh vegetables put together with various flavourings.

Yoghurt in its whisked or liquidised form constitutes the medium for all raitas or yoghurt salads. In the West the emphasis for these salads is usually on fruit. We in India use all sorts of vegetables for yoghurt salads.

Pickles like chutneys and raitas are also an integral part of the Indian kitchen. For our climate, pungent and hot pickles are said to facilitate digestion, the souring ingredients for these being mustard. In the Western kitchen though, the use of vinegar is more common as the diet consists mainly of meats that are digested well by vinegar. The recipes given here use both ingredients.

Green Coriander Chutney

One of the most widely consumed chutneys in India. It is popular with most vegetarian and non-vegetarian dishes.

Green coriander chopped	1½ cups
Green chillies	2
Lemon juice	2 tbsp
Salt	to taste

Put all the ingredients into a wet grinder and blend to a semi-liquid paste. If you like you can add a pinch of sugar to improve the flavour.

Green Mint Chutney

A delicious chutney that goes specially well with mince kababs of all kinds.

Green mint leaves chopped	1 cup
Green coriander chopped	1/4 cup
Green chillies	4
Garlic cloves	2
Lemon juice	3 tbsp
Salt	to taste

Put all the ingredients into a wet grinder and blend to a semi-liquid paste.

Peanut Chutney

Peanuts are used in kitchens all over India, the most interesting fact being that they are used differently in each. They may be used raw, roasted, chopped, or pasted. Peanuts are wonderfully versatile, and nutritious too.

Peanuts roasted	1/2 cup
Green chillies	2
Lemon juice	1 tbsp
Ginger chopped	1 tsp
Green coriander chopped	1 tbsp
Water	2 tbsp
Salt	to taste

Put all the ingredients apart from the water into a wet grinder. Blend them to a granular consistency, adding little water at a time, and making sure the end result is not pasty.

Mustard Chutney

A recipe that was inspired by my late father's love for mustard.

Mustard powder (WeikField's)	1 cup
Turmeric powder	2 tsp
Ascorbic acid tablets* powdered	3
Acetic acid glacial	1 tsp
Groundnut oil	1 tbsp
Water	1/2 cup
Salt	to taste

Mix mustard, turmeric, salt and ascorbic acid in a glass container. Add water and stir slowly with a wooden spoon. Cover the container and keep for twenty to twenty-five minutes. Add acetic acid and stir again. Check for salt. Put the chutney in a bottle and pour the oil on top. Use after twenty-four hours. Store in a cool place.

* 500 mg each

Tomato Chutney

Here is the Indian 'Tomato Ketchup'.

Tomatoes chopped	2 cups
Ginger paste	2 tsp
Garlic paste	1 tsp
Green coriander chopped	2 tbsp
Red chilli powder	2 tsp
Sugar	1 tbsp
Salt	to taste

Chop the tomatoes fine. Mix all the
ingredients together and cook on a
slow fire in a heavy bottom pan, till a
saucy consistency is reached. No oil
is required for cooking. Remove from
fire, cool and serve.

Til Chutney

*Til or sesame is very popular in India.
Its distinctive flavour does not permit it
to blend with all foods, but as a chutney
it goes well with many recipes.*

Sesame seeds roasted	1 tbsp
Green chillies	3
Mint leaves	1/2 cup
Onion large	1
Garlic clove	1
Tamarind pulp	2 tbsp
Salt	to taste

Roast the sesame seeds and grind
coarsely. Put these along with all the
other ingredients into a wet grinder
and blend to a semi-liquid paste.

Mint Yoghurt Chutney

*A speciality of North India using a
different souring in the form of dried
pomegranate seeds. These seeds first
used in north-west India and Kandahar
in Afghanistan, impart a unique taste
and texture to the chutney.*

Green mint leaves	1 cup
Yoghurt	1/2 cup
Pomegranate seeds	1½ tbsp
Lemon juice	1 tsp
Sugar	1 tsp
Salt	to taste

Pound the pomegranate seeds with the
yoghurt. Put all the ingredients in a
wet grinder and grind to a granular
consistency.

Chilli Garlic Chutney

*The two most popular flavours in
Indian cooking. To me chillies without
garlic, are like eggs without salt.*

Red chillies whole*	8
Garlic cloves	20
Lemon juice	2 tsp
Salt	to taste

Put all the ingredients into a wet
grinder and blend to a semi-liquid
paste.

* For a really hot chutney add more
chillies.

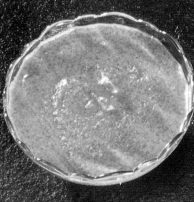

Mustard Chutney

Chilli Garlic Chutney

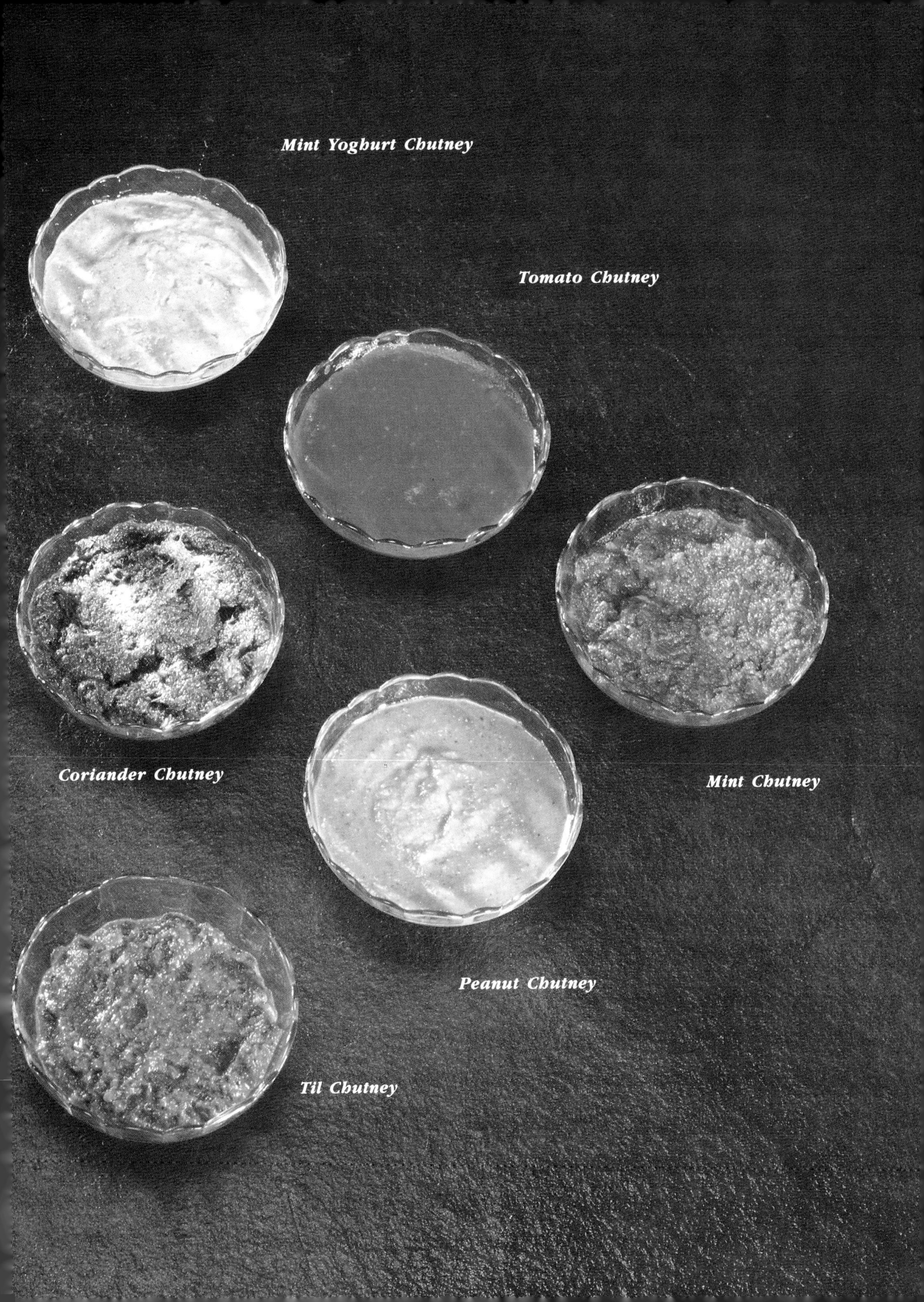

Mint Yoghurt Chutney

Tomato Chutney

Coriander Chutney

Mint Chutney

Peanut Chutney

Til Chutney

Peanut Cabbage Relish

*Here is a totally different way of
using peanuts. This relish goes well
with almost all tandoori recipes.*

Peanuts roasted (pounded)	1/4 cup
Medium cabbage minced	1
Green coriander minced	1 tbsp
Green chillies minced	2
Lemon juice	1/4 cup
Sugar	2 tsp
Salt	to taste

Coarsely grind the peanuts. Mix a little
salt in the cabbage and set aside for ten
minutes. Drain the cabbage. Add the
rest of the ingredients, mix well and
serve.

White Radish Relish

*Winter, the ideal time for eating
outdoors, is also when red and white
radish is at its best.*

White radish grated	2 cups
Tender leaves of	
white radish chopped fine	few
Lemon juice	3 tbsp
Green chillies minced	to taste
Salt	to taste

Put the radish in cold water for
ten minutes. Drain and put in the
refrigerator for ten minutes. Add the
rest of the ingredients and serve.

Cucumber Relish

A very refreshing summer relish.

Medium cucumbers	3
Spring onions	3
Green chillies minced	1 tbsp
Dill leaves minced	1 tsp
Lemon juice	1/4 cup
Salt	to taste

Cut cucumbers and spring onions into
matchstick slivers. Put them in cold
water for ten minutes. Strain and put in
the refrigerator for ten minutes. Add the
rest of the ingredients and serve.

Cachumbar Relish

Cachumbar — the name means to make a mix of a number of things. That is literally what we do in this recipe. Simple and excellent with tandoori meats.

Onions medium	2
Tomatoes medium	2
Cucumber medium	2
Green chillies chopped	2
Lemons	2
Salt	to taste

Dice the onions, tomatoes and cucumbers. Add salt and green chillies. Mix well. Squeeze the lemon and serve.

Mixed Green Relish

This simple and uncomplicated preparation is as full of flavour as the fresh spring air.

Capsicum	2
Spring onions with leaves	4
Cucumbers	2
Mint leaves chopped	few
Black pepper powder	1 tsp
Lemon juice	1/4 cup
Salt	to taste

Cut the capsicums, spring onion and cucumber into matchstick slivers. Put the greens in cold water for ten minutes, drain and put in the refrigerator for ten minutes. Add the rest of the ingredients and serve.

Onion and Tomato Yoghurt Salad

The two yoghurt salads that really go well with the meaty kitchen are onion yoghurt salad, and onion and tomato yoghurt salad. I am giving the recipe for the second one. The first is made in the same way but without tomatoes.

Onions medium	2
Tomatoes medium	2
Green chillies	4
Yoghurt*	2 cups
Salt	to taste

Dice the onions and tomatoes, chop the green chillies and mix them together. Add the salt and set aside for ten minutes. Whip the yoghurt a little, add it to the above ingredients.

For other raitas, substitute the onions and tomatoes with any of the following boiled potatoes, cucumber, radish, carrots, mint, aubergines batter fried in split chickpea flour etc. The green chillies can be substitued with red chillies and some roasted and ground cumin can be sprinkled on top. These are just some of the possibilities. You can always create your own raitas.

* Do not use water

Pickled Onions

In the good old days when Moti Mahal was the only place that served tandoori food in Delhi, I would wait eagerly for the pickled onions. Now they are popular all over the world. Here is my own tried and tested recipe.

Small onions* (white)	10
White Vinegar	1 cup
Sugar	4 tbsp
Salt	1 tsp

Peel the small onions. With a knife make a small cut on top of each onion, going through half way to the centre. Dissolve the sugar in the vinegar and add the salt. Put the onions in this mixture and keep in a glass bottle. It takes two to three days to mature in warm climates and slightly longer in cooler climates.

* In case white onions are not available, take a small size of the ordinary pink onions, remove two layers of outer skin and you will get good results.

Mixed Vegetable Pickle

One of my favourite rai-wala achars, this pickle goes with a wide variety of Indian foods.

Carrots cut diagonally	2 cups
Turnips cut diagonally	1 cup
Cauliflower (small florets)	2 cups
Red chilli powder	2 tbsp
Turmeric powder	1 tsp
Indian brown mustard powdered	1/4 cup
Salt	to taste
Water	8 cups

Boil the water in a large vessel. When it reaches boiling point turn off the heat and put the vegetables in it. Cover and leave for ten minutes. Drain well. Mix the dry ingredients with the vegetables in another dish. Cover and leave for twenty-four hours. Turn the vegetables into a bottle or glass jar and keep in a warm area for three to four days till the mustard has matured, and the vegetables have got a tangy flavour.

In India this pickle is usually made in winter when these vegetables are in abundance.

Gherkin Dill Pickle

Gherkins are a small variety of cucumbers grown specially for pickling.

Gherkins	7
Caraway seeds	1 tsp
Dill greens chopped	1 tbsp
White vinegar	1 cup
Sugar	1/2 cup
Salt	to taste

Wash and dry the gherkins. With a knife make a fine slit through the centre of each gherkin. Mix all the rest of the ingredients and put the gherkins in this. They will take three to five days to pickle, depending on the climate.

Glossary of Names
and Weight Equivalents for Solids

English	Indian	Tea spoon (grams)	Table spoon (grams)	cup (grams)
Almonds	Badam	3.5	10.0	150
skinned & chopped,	chheela hua			
Aniseed	Sonf choti	3.0	9.0	145
Apricot chopped	Khubani kati hui	3.5	10.0	150
Asafoetida				
(compounded powder)	Hing	1.3	4.0	—
Baking powder	Baking powder	3.5	10.0	—
Basil (Indian)	Tulsi			
leaves chopped	kati hui	1.0	2.0	30
Basil (Sweet)	Ban tulsi			
leaves chopped	kati hui	1.0	2.0	30
Bay leaf*	Tej patta			
Black peppercorns	Kali mirch sabut	2.8	8.0	—
Black pepper powder	Kali mirch pissi hui	3.5	10.0	—
Bread crumbs	Double roti ka choora	1.8	5.3	85
Butter	Makhan	5.0	15.0	240
Caraway seed	Shah zira	2.5	7.5	—
Cardamom brown seed	Bari elaichi	2.3	6.8	—
Cardamom green seed	Choti elaichi	2.5	7.5	—
Carum seed	Ajwain	2.0	6.3	—
Carum powder	Ajwain pissi hui	2.8	8.0	—
Cashewnuts pounded	Kaju kuta hua	2.5	7.5	120
Charcoal tablets	Khanay wala			
powder*	koela	1.0	3.0	—
Chickpea flour	Besan	2.5	7.5	125
Chickpea split	Channa dal	5.0	15.0	250
Chillies green minced	Hari mirch bareek kati	2.0	6.0	—
Chillies red powder	Lal mirch pissi hui	2.0	6.0	—
Chillies red pounded	Bukni	1.7	5.0	—
Chironji chopped	*Buchanania latifolia*†	2.5	7.5	120
Cinnamon powder	Dalchini pissi hui	2.8	8.5	—
Clove powder	Laung pissi hui	2.5	7.5	—
Coriander green	Hara dhanya			
minced	bareek kata	2.0	5.0	80

† Botanical name   * Use charcoal tablets of good grade quality only

English	Indian	Tea spoon (grams)	Table spoon (grams)	Cup (grams)
Coriander seed	Dhania sabut	1.8	5.0	80
Coriander powder	Dhania pissa hua	2	6	95
Cornflakes powdered	Cornflakes ka atta	1.8	5.5	90
Corn flour	Nisasta	2	6	95
Cumin seed	Zira	3	8.5	135
Cumin powder	Zira pissa hua	3.5	10	160
Curry leaves chopped	Curry patta	1	2	30
Fennel	Sonf moti	2.5	7.5	—
Fenugreek green leaves	Hari methi	1	2	30
Fenugreek seed	Methi dana	4.3	12.5	—
Fenugreek powder	Methi pissi hui	3.0	8.3	—
Five spices (Indian)	Panch phoran*	4.0	12.0	—
Figs chopped	Anjeer kati hui	3.5	10.0	150
Four kernels	Char magaz**	3.5	10.0	150
Fox gram	Moth	5.0	15.0	250
Garlic minced	Lahsan bareek kata hua	2.5	7.5	—
Ginger minced	Adrak bareek kati hui	2.5	7.5	—
Ginger dry powder	Sonth pissi hui	2.0	6.0	—
Indian cottage cheese loose	Paneer dhila	2.0	6.0	100
Kachri powder	*Cucumis pubescens*†	2.0	6.0	—
Mace powdered	Javitri pissi hui	2.0	6.0	—
Mint leaves chopped	Pudina kata hua	0.8	2.5	30
Mustard black seed	Sarson	3.0	9.0	—
Mustard brown seed	Rai	3.8	11	—
Mustard powder	Compounded mixture	2.0	6.0	—
Nigella seed	Kalonji	2.8	8.3	—
Nutmeg powder	Jaiphal pissa hua	2.0	6.0	—
Onion minced	Piyaz bareek kata hua	2.5	7.5	120
Peanuts pounded	Moongphali kuti hui	2.5	7.5	120

* Five spices or panch phoran is a mixture of mustard, nigella, fenugreek, fennel and cumin seeds in equal propotions.

** Four kernels or char magaz is a mixture of cucumber, melon, musk melon and gourd seeds in equal proportions.

† Botanical names.

English	Indian	Tea spoon (grams)	Table spoon (grams)	Cup (grams)
Pinenuts pounded	Chilgoza kuta hua	2.5	7.5	120
Pistachio nuts pounded	Pista kuta hua	2.5	7.5	120
Pomegranate seed	Anardana	3.0	10.0	—
Poppy seed	Khaskhas	3.5	10.0	—
Raisins	Khismish	3.0	10.0	150
Ratanjyot crushed	*Onosma echioides*†	1.0	3.0	—
Raw mango powder	Amchoor pissa hua	2.5	7.5	
Roasted bengal gram flour	Bhoonay channe ka atta	3.0	9.0	150
Rose petals	Gulab ki patti	1.0	3.0	50
Saffron	Kesar	0.5	1.5	—
Salt	Namak	5.0	15.0	
Semolina	Sooji	5.0	14.0	180
Sesame seed (white)	Til safed	3.0	9.0	145
Silverfoil*	Chandi ka wark			
Spring onion minced	Hari pyaz bareek kata	2.5	7.5	120
Sprouted green lentil	Sabat mung phoota hua	—	—	60
Sultana	Manakka	2.0	6.0	100
Thandai mix**		—	10.0	150
Tofu	Soyabean ka panir			
Turmeric powder	Haldi pissi hui	3.5	10.0	—
Walnut pounded	Akhrot kuta hua	2.5	7.5	120
Water melon seed	Tarbooz ka beej	2.5	7.5	120
White flour	Maida	3.5	10.0	150
White pepper powder	Safaid mirch pissi hui	3.5	10.0	—
Whole wheat flour	Atta	4.0	12.0	200
Yeast dry	Khamir	2.0	6.0	—
Yeast fresh	Taza khamir	5.0	15.0	—

* Generally purchased in numbers

** Thandai mix measures for approximately 1/2 cup are given below

Poppy seeds	2½ tbs	Cardamom (seed only)	1 tsp (6 or 7)
Black peppercorns	1/2 tbs	Almonds skinned	20
Rose petals dry	1½ tbs	Aniseed	2 tsp
Shelled seeds of cucumber, melon, musk melon, gourd	2 tbs		

† Botanical name

Glossary of Names
and Volume Equivalents for Liquids

English	Indian	Measures
Butter (melted)	Makhan	
Butter milk	Khatti lassi	
Butter oil	Ghee	
Double cream	Malai	
Honey	Shahad	All liquid measures
Lemon juice	Nimbu ka ras	are as follows
Oil	Tel	1 teaspoon = 5 ml
Screwpine essence	Keora	1 tablespoon = 15 ml
Yoghurt	Dahi	1 cup = 240 ml
Yoghurt hung	Bandhi dahi	
Tamarind pulp	Imly bhigi hui	
Water	Pani	
White vinegar	Sirka	

Glossary of Names
and Volume Equivalents for Pastes

English	Indian	Measures
Almond paste	Badam pissa hua	
Coriander green paste	Hara dhania pissa hua	All paste measures
Garlic paste	Lahsan pissa hua	are as follows
Ginger paste	Adrak pissi hui	1 teaspoon = 5 ml
Onion paste	Piyaz pissa hua	1 tablespoon = 15 ml
Raw fig paste	Kachi anjeer pissi hui	1 cup = 240 ml
Raw papaya paste	Kacha papita pissa hua	
Raw pineapple paste	Kacha ananas pissa hua	

Index

A

B

C

F

L

Additional Acknowledgements

Photographs

Times of India, 6
Archaeological Survey of India, 18, 25,
   26, 28
Margrith Sengupta, 28, 53 (Pakistan), 56,
   61, 63, 67
D.P. Mohley, 34
Welcomgroup Maurya Sheraton, 36-37
Karla Schefter, 57, 58, 59, 60
S.C. Shekhar, 68, 69, 105
Ranmal Singh Jhala, 246

Illustrations
Ranmal Singh Jhala
Umade Jhala, 107